ADVERTISEMENT.

I BEGAN to write this little book, while Pastor of the Westminster Presbyterian Church, Baltimòre, preaching as I wrote. One or two passages as to their substance, and several as to their form, need this explanation. These memorials of a joyful ministry I have found it convenient and pleasant to retain, in rewriting everything with what pains I could bestow.

BLIND BARTIMEUS;

OR,

THE STORY

OF

A SIGHTLESS SINNER

AND

HIS GREAT PHYSICIAN.

BY

REV. WILLIAM J. HOGE,

PROFESSOR IN THE UNION THEOLOGICAL SEMINARY, PRINCE EDWARD, VIRGINIA.

NEW YORK:

SHELDON & COMPANY.

No. 115 NASSAU STREET.

1859.

TO

The Glory of the Lord Jesus Christ,

THIS HUMBLE ATTEMPT

TO COMMEND TO SOULS IN BLINDNESS

HIS GRACE AND POWER,

Is Dedicated.

BLIND BARTIMEUS.

MATTHEW'S ACCOUNT.

xx. 29–34.

And as they departed from Jericho a great multitude followed Him. And behold, two blind men sitting by the way side, when they heard that Jesus passed by, cried out, saying, Have mercy on us, O Lord, thou Son of David. And the multitude rebuked them, because they should hold their peace: but they cried the more, saying, Have mercy on us, O Lord, thou Son of David. And Jesus stood still, and called them, and said, What will ye that I shall do unto you? They say unto Him, Lord, that our eyes may be opened. So Jesus had compassion on them, and touched their eyes: and immediately their eyes received sight, and they followed Him.

MARK'S ACCOUNT.

x. 46–52.

And they came to Jericho: and as He went out of Jericho with His disciples, and a great number of people, blind Bartimeus, the son of Timæus, sat by the highway side begging. And when he heard that it was Jesus of Nazareth, he began to cry out, and say, Jesus, thou Son of David, have mercy on me. And many charged him that he should hold his peace: but he cried the more a great deal, Thou Son of David, have mercy on me. And Jesus stood still, and commanded him to be called: and they call the blind man, saying unto him, Be of good comfort, rise; He calleth thee. And he, casting away his garment, rose, and came to Jesus. And Jesus answered and said unto him, What wilt thou that I should do unto thee? The blind man said unto Him, Lord, that I might receive my sight. And Jesus said unto him, Go thy way; thy faith hath made thee whole. And immediately he received his sight, and followed Jesus in the way.

LUKE'S ACCOUNT.

xviii. 35–43.

And it came to pass, that as He was come nigh unto Jericho, a certain blind man sat by the way side begging; and hearing the multitude pass by, he asked what it meant. And they told him, that Jesus of Nazareth passeth by. And he cried, saying, Jesus, thou Son of David, have mercy on me. And they which went before rebuked him, that he should hold his peace: but he cried so much the more, Thou Son of David, have mercy on me. And Jesus stood and commanded him to be brought unto Him: and when he was come near, He asked him, saying, What wilt thou that I shall do unto thee? And he said, Lord, that I may receive my sight. And Jesus said unto him, Receive thy sight: thy faith hath saved thee. And immediately he received his sight, and followed him, glorifying God: and all the people, when they saw it, gave praise unto God.

THE FULL NARRATIVE,

COMPILED FROM THE THREE EVANGELISTS.

And they came to Jericho: and as He went out of Jericho with His disciples and a great number of people, blind Bartimeus, the son of Timæus, sat by the highway side begging. And hearing the multitude pass by, he asked what it meant; and they told him that Jesus of Nazareth passeth by. And when he heard that it was Jesus of Nazareth, he began to cry out, and say, "Jesus, Thou Son of David, have mercy on me! O Lord, Thou Son of David, have mercy on me!" And many—they which went before—rebuked him, and charged him that he should hold his peace. But he cried the more, the more a great deal, "O Lord, Thou Son of David, have mercy on me!"

And Jesus stood still, and called him. He also commanded him to be called, and even to be brought unto Him.

And they call the blind man, saying unto him, "Be of good comfort! Rise! He calleth thee!"

And he, casting away his garment, rose and came to Jesus.

And when he was come near, Jesus asked him, saying, "What wilt thou that I should do unto thee?" The blind man answered and said unto Him, "Lord, that I might receive my sight!" So Jesus had compassion, and touched his eyes, and said unto him, "Receive thy sight! Go thy way: thy faith hath saved thee."

And immediately he received his sight, and followed Jesus in the way, glorifying God. And all the people, when they saw it, gave praise unto God.

Introduction.

MATTHEW, Mark, and Luke all give this story, but with some variations. Indeed, there are two things which look like contradictions. In Luke we read that the miracle was wrought as Jesus was come nigh unto Jericho, while Matthew and Mark agree that it was as He went out of the city. Again, Matthew says two blind men were healed, while Mark and Luke speak of but one.

Matthew Henry gives a very short answer to the second difficulty. "If there were two," he says, "there was one." In this he but expresses, in his quaint way, the well-known rule of interpretation that, where several historians narrate the same event, it is no contradiction for one to give incidents about which others are silent. If, indeed, the number is an essential element in the narrative, it must be given with accuracy. If a general won a battle with ten thousand men, he would be a false historian who should say he won it with five thousand. But if one historian should tell us of a great captain's fighting two battles the same day, it would be no impeachment of his veracity, if another chronicler should tell us of but one of these battles. One might be so insignificant that it would be lost in the greatness of the other; or it might not concern the special design of one of the narratives; or any similar reason might prevail. And surely the number is not the great thing here. Christ healed such multitudes that, in any given case, it is a small matter to the gospel narrative whether He healed one or more. Amid the gracious prodigality of His miracles, there may well be a noble negligence, on the part of His biographers, as to the exact number He cured. The great thing is, that He healed at all maladies incurable by any power but divine. And one Evangelist might often have special reasons (as Mark, perhaps, in this case,) for relating only the more conspicuous and important cure. Why should any one feel a difficulty when Luke simply tells us that, when

Christ was near Jericho, He wrought so illustrious a miracle as giving sight to a blind man; and Mark, writing, perhaps, to some who would be especially interested to know this, says that "the son of Timeus, blind Bartimeus"—a man widely known, it may be—on that day received his sight; while Matthew tells us that, on that blessed day, *two* souls were made glad by the healing word of Christ?

Thus the seeming contradiction vanishes, and turns rather into a confirmation of the truth and independence of the narratives. An impostor would have avoided this.

The other difficulty remains. Matthew and Mark say the cure was performed as He left the city; Luke, as He came near it. How shall these statements be reconciled?

Several solutions have been proposed, of which I think the following is the best.

One blind man cried to Christ as He was going into Jericho, but was not cured until, joining himself to a companion in blindness, they cried together to Him as He was leaving the city. Luke, however, having *begun* the narrative where the first man cried out, carries it on to the end without interruption. All historians do this. They constantly relate events which run through months or even years, never breaking the thread of their narrative by even an allusion, meantime, to whatever else is taking place. In *this* case the story of the blind man begins on one side of the city, as Christ is going in, and ends on the other, as He is going out; while *in* the city His visit to Zaccheus is to be related.[1] Now three courses are possible to the narrator. He may begin with what took place as Christ drew near the city, and tell that story to its end, and then tell what occurred in the city. This is what Luke does. Or commencing with what began on one side of the city and ended on the other, he may suddenly check his narrative to tell of Zaccheus, and then go on again with his account of the blind men. But this would sacrifice our pleasure in the separate and undisturbed beauty of each picture, merely to secure what Trench well calls a "painful accuracy." Or, finally, he may refuse to begin the first story until he comes where the most important

[1] Luke, xix. 1–10.

part of it took place, namely, the actual healing of the men, as Christ was leaving Jericho. This is what Matthew and Mark do.

Like the other, this seeming discrepancy lies too much on the surface for the work of an impostor. He would have made his three narratives harmonize more easily, lest any should reject them. If the Gospels were cunningly devised fables, there would be contradictions indeed, but not like these. They would not lie on the surface, readily detected, and avoided as readily; but in the very depth and heart of things, hard perhaps to discern, and impossible to reconcile. Gaining easy triumphs for a time, such narratives would be utterly overwhelmed at length. But true men write with an unconscious variety and naturalness, which looks at first like contradiction, but which, more closely questioned, gives out a deeper testimony for independence and integrity.

I wish now to say something of the relation of Christ's miracles to things more purely spiritual, that I may at once guard and justify the use I intend to make of the record of the healing of blind Bartimeus.

1. I do not suppose a double sense, as it is called, in which the words have, besides the obvious meaning which we would give them in other books, a hidden, spiritual meaning, which we must task our ingenuity to search out. This theory is without foundation, and opens a wide door for every fancy and heresy. The words have but one sense. They are simply a record of a miracle of healing.

2. But the miracles of the New Testament are miracles of grace. They are not mere signs and wonders. Power is not their chief element. They are essentially redemptive,—works of God's forgiving and restoring love. They are not meant merely to astonish, much less to terrify. They bless, and curse not; bringing no fire from heaven[1] but that which relumes the extinguished lamp of life; and dealing with leprosy, blindness, and pain, only that they may drive them away. They are not even mere proofs of a divine mission. They do not, like the Magi, come from some far-off

[1] Luke, ix. 54–56.

region, and having offered their incense to Christ, pass away again to be seen no more.[1] They all speak the language of Canaan,[2] and, with heavenly tongue, bear witness that Jesus is the Son of God,[3] while, as sons, they have the freedom of His house, and abide with Him forever.[4] They prove His mission chiefly as they themselves are a part of it. They establish His Messiahship by exemplifying it. To men doubting and perishing they bring heavy clusters from that Eshcol, whose reality and surpassing fruitfulness they would demonstrate.[5]

Ages ago, Augustine expressed this thought with much beauty. Speaking of the miracles, he says, "Our Lord and Saviour Jesus Christ is the Physician of our eternal health, and to this end He took the weakness of our nature, that our weakness might not last forever." And Trench finely calls them "miracles of the Incarnation,—of the Son of God, who had taken our flesh, and taking would heal it." Thus is every miracle of Christ, as he says

[1] Mat., ii. 1, 11, 12. [2] Isa., xix. 18. [3] John, v. 36; xx. 30, 31. [4] John, viii. 35. [5] Numb., xiii. 23.

again, "an index and prophecy of the inner work of man's deliverance." "In each of them the word of salvation is incorporated in an act of salvation."

Sin has cursed not only man's soul but his body,[1] and there is a fearful analogy between the diseases, distortions, and ruins of the body, and the deformities and corruptions of the soul. Therefore when we see our Saviour manifesting His healing grace in repairing the ravages which the Destroyer has made on man's body, we can not fail also to have new and deeper insight into His redeeming work on man's spirit. And it would be wonderful, when this is so, if some of the records of these gracious healings should not be, throughout, aptest *illustrations* of a sinner's restoration by the power and grace of Jesus.

3. Again, great principles are often contained in these narratives, which are of universal application. If we see that the vilest have free access to Jesus; that He heals the wretched without price, of His own pure grace; that importunity ever gains its point; that every

[1] Gen., iii. 16–19.

thing depends on faith; that the largest faith is ever most applauded and most blessed; that no disease is beyond His power; that these and many such things are true in these miracles of bodily healing, then do we as surely know that we may rest confidently upon them, when we go to Him in the deeper unworthiness of sin, and with the more awful maladies of our souls![1]

[1] Mat., ix. 6, 35; Luke, vii. 19–23.

BLIND BARTIMEUS.

I.

"And they came to Jericho; and as He went out of Jericho with His disciples, and a great number of people, blind Bartimeus, the son of Timeus, sat by the highway side, begging."

WHAT a sad sight is this! A blind beggar sitting by the way side! His clothes are tattered and filthy. His face is burned by many a sun, and browned by many a rude wind, and furrowed with many a wrinkle, making channels for tears, and writing histories of sorrow. His hand still grasps his long staff,—his only support and guide, as every morning he gropes his way from his hovel to his accustomed haunt on this high road to Jerusalem. He has taken his seat on the well-worn stone under the palm-tree, and now he waits patiently in the grateful shade for some passing traveler from whom he may ask an alms; for on the chance pittance of charity he must live. Unhappy man, if he has a wife and children depending on this slender, precarious support! More unhappy, if he must bear his dark life alone!

Is he man as God made him? Is that the divine image? Is he possessor and lord of the world? Where is the dignity and might, the kingly dominion and grandeur of the earth's ancient ruler? O how changed, how fallen, how lost! Poor Bartimeus, sad picture of all thy race! In thee I see myself and every brother, in our estate of nature. Image of the unregenerate man,—blind, poor, a beggar, and helpless alike in wretchedness and ruin!

Shrink not, O believer, this is what thou wast. Shrink not, O unbeliever, this is what thou art.

Nay, the redeemed friends of Jesus will not shrink. They have long been accustomed to gaze on this sad likeness of themselves, and being now the children of adoption through grace, they still gaze upon it to renew repentance and humility, and to adore Him who has changed it to joy and peace and eternal hope.

And let all in whom Jesus Christ hath wrought no miracle of spiritual healing, look steadily on this picture, and hear the voice of God saying, Thou art the man![1]

I.—HIS BLINDNESS.

Bartimeus is blind. And what is that? The eyes of his body are out. He sees no light, or color, or form. I do not say his mind perceives nothing, or his heart feels nothing. His wits may be keen and his affections lively. I only say his bodily eyes can not see. They are blind.

And what is true of the eyes of his body, is true, O sinner, of the eyes of your soul. He could not see the natural world, and you can not see the spiritual world. The eye of sense may be bright in you, and its vision clear. The eye of the mind may be bright in you, and *its* vision clear. But the eye of your soul has been put out. It is blind.

[1] 2 Sam., xii. 7.

You see I speak of three kinds of blindness. The eye of the body may be out, and we have no name for the result but blindness. The eye of the intellect may be out, and we name the result idiocy. We say the man is a fool. The eye of the soul may be out, and God names the result wickedness. He calls the man a sinner.

Think of Bartimeus. He rose this morning, and his wife blessed him, his children climbed his knees and kissed him. They ministered to his wants. They led him a little way by the hand. But he did not see them. He knew of them, but he could not behold them. Their smiles or beauty were nothing to him,—he was blind.

Think of yourself, O sinner. You rose this morning, and the eye of your heavenly Father looked upon you. His hand led you, His power guarded you, His goodness blessed you. But your soul did not see Him. A vague idea that God had done it all may have occurred to you, but it had no vividness. He was no blessed reality to you. You saw not the lineaments of a Father,—the loving eye, the benignant smile. You saw nothing,—your soul was blind.

Think again of Bartimeus. He went abroad, and the rich valley of the Jordan spread out before him. The stately palms rose toward heaven, and waved their feathery tops in the early breeze. The gardens of balsam were clothed in their delicate spring[1] verdure, and Jericho sat in the midst of these vernal glories, deserving its name,—Jericho, the place of fragrance, deserving its frequent description among the ancient writers,—the City of Palms. And high above all was the blue sky, bending over as if to embrace and bless so much loveliness of earth; and the great sun, filling earth and sky and balmy air with glory.

But what was all this to Bartimeus? It might have been narrow and black for aught he could tell. It *was* an utter blank, a dreadful gloom to him. All was night, black, black night, with no star.

Why was it so to him, when to others it was splendor and joy? Ah! he was blind.

[1] For it was at this season that Christ was then going to Jerusalem.

Unregenerate man, think again of yourself. You went abroad this morning, on an earth once cursed,[1] as of old Jericho had been,[2] but spared and blessed by redeeming mercy, even as Jericho was that day blessed by the presence and healing grace of Jesus. Around you, too, was spread a world of spiritual beauty. The walls, and bulwarks, and stately palaces of the city of our God were before you. The rose of Sharon, the lily of the valley, the vine, the palm, the olive, and the fig-tree all stood about you in the garden of the Lord. Through them flowed the river of life, reflecting skies more high and clear than the azure of summer mornings ever imaged, and lit to its measureless depth by a sun more glorious than ever poured splendor even upon Eden, in our poor world's ancient prime. You walked forth amid all this beauty, and many saw it,—none perfectly, yet some very blessedly,—but you saw nothing. You see nothing now. Nay, you can not see it. Strain your blind soul as you will, you can not see it. What I have said of it seems to you but

[1] Gen., iii. 17, 18; Rom., viii. 20. [2] Josh., vi. 17, 26.

a phantasy and rhapsody, although I say it on the awful authority of God in His Holy Word, and the experience of unnumbered children of His, who are witnesses that what I say is true, and for their witness would dare to die. Why then do you not see it? Ah! the eye of the soul is out,—you are blind.

I see a beautiful mother gaze anxiously on her babe. She is trying a fearful experiment. She stretches out her arms to it, beseeches it with loving looks, holds out sparkling jewels to it, and flashes them before its eyes in the very sunshine at the open window. But the little eyes move not, or move aimlessly, and turn vacantly away. And she cries out in anguish, "Oh my poor child is blind!"

And now I understand why even tender children turn away from Christ, seeing no beauty in Him that they should desire Him,[1] and caring nothing for all His smiles or tears, or offers of the rich jewelry of heaven. They *see* nothing of it all. They are blind, born blind.

I have read of a man of old to whom God

[1] Isaiah, liii. 2.

had given great might, for dignity and honor and the redemption of his enslaved country, who made unwieldy mirth for thousands of scoffing Philistines. He had come from grinding in their prison, where slaves were his masters, and now he made sport in open day, while the uncircumcised triumphed and jeered. But he saw neither the dungeon nor the day, for they had put out his eyes,—Samson was blind.

And now I understand how men can make themselves the slaves and scoff of devils, as they rattle their chains and dance in their fetters, and play the fool with the high powers God has given them for usefulness to their fellows, and their own glory, honor and immortality. In the daily drudgeries of mere worldly business, and the occasional levities of mere worldly amusement, they are alike represented by fallen and degraded Samson in his blindness.

I once saw a man walk along the edge of a precipice as if it were a plain. For any thing he knew, it was a plain, and safe. He was calm and fearless, not because there was no danger, but because he was blind.

And who can not now understand how men so wise, so cautious in most things, can go so securely, so carelessly, even so gaily on, as if every thing were safe for eternity, while snares and pit-falls are all about them, and death may be just at hand, and the next step may send them down the infinite abyss! O, we see it, we see it,—they are blind!

A blind man is more taken up with what he holds in his hand, than with mountains, ocean, sun, or stars. He feels this; but those he can neither touch nor see.

And now it is plain why unconverted men undervalue doctrine, saying, that "it is no matter what a man believes, so his heart is right;" that "one doctrine is as good as another, and for that matter, no doctrines are good for much;" and that "they don't believe in doctrinal preaching at any rate." They, forsooth, they! blind worms, pronouncing contemptuously of the stupendous heights and glories of God's revelation, where alone we learn what we are to believe concerning Him, and what duty He requires of us.

It is plain too why they see no preciousness

in the promises, no glory in Christ, no beauty in holiness, no grandeur in the work of redemption; why they make a mock at sin, despise God's threatenings, brave His wrath, make light of the blood of Christ, jest at death, and rush headlong on certain perdition. They are blind. So the Scripture speaks. There are blind people that have eyes.[1] Having the understanding darkened, being alienated from the life of God, through the ignorance that is in them, because of the blindness of their heart.[2] So there is such a thing as heart blindness, as well as blindness of the bodily eye.

Unconverted men often say, "If these things are so, if they are so clear and great, why can not we see them?" And there is no answer to be given but this, Ye are blind.

"But we *want* to see them. If they are real, they are our concern as well as yours. Oh, that some preacher would come, who had power to make us see them!"

Poor souls, there is no such preacher, and you need not wait for him. Let him gather

[1] Isa., xliii. 8. [2] Eph., iv. 18.

God's light as he will, he can but pour it on blind eyes. A burning-glass will condense sunbeams into a focus of brightness; and if a blind eye be put there, not a whit will it see, though it be consumed. Light is the remedy for darkness, not blindness.

Neither will strong powers of understanding on your part, serve. The great Earl of Chatham once went with a pious friend to hear Mr. Cecil. The sermon was on the Spirit's agency in the hearts of believers. As they were coming from church, the mighty statesman confessed that he could not understand it at all, and asked his friend if he supposed that any one in the house could. "Why yes," said he, "there were many plain, unlettered women and some children there, who understood every word of it, and heard it with joy."

Ah, hapless souls, ye complain against the gospel, that it is hidden from you, as if that were *its* fault. And now I must bring forth a dreadful Scripture which will open the mystery of your inability to understand it. O it is a fearful word, which ought to make your ears tingle and your heart freeze with terror as you hear it;—If our gospel be hid, it is hid to them that are lost, in whom the god of this world hath blinded the minds of them that believe not, lest the light of the glorious gospel of Christ, who is the image of God, should shine unto them.[1] The gospel is real and glorious, and is all the while shining on in its own divine splendor; but you are blind. Satan, the old liar and murderer,[2] has blinded you *lest* you should see this blessed gospel and be saved. And you are lost, lost already. There is your dreadful condition, and *therefore* you can not see the gospel!

Let the people of God no more wonder then at the clamors of infidels against the Scriptures. Would you heed a blind man criticising pictures, or raving against your summer skies? If he denies that the sun has brightness, or the mountains grandeur, will you believe him? And if a hundred blind men should all declare that they can not see the stars, and argue learnedly that there can be no stars, and

[1] 2 Cor., iv. 3, 4. [2] John, viii. 44.

then grow witty and laugh at you as star-gazers, would the midnight heavens be less glorious to you? When these men had thus satisfactorily demonstrated their blindness, would not the mighty works of God still prove their bright reality to your rejoicing vision? Would they not still declare His glory and show His handiwork?[1]

And shall the spiritually blind be more trusted? Shall they be spiritual guides? No, the weakest believer who has seen that the Lord is gracious,[2] seen any preciousness in the promises, any beauty in Christ, any glory in the Scriptures, may cling to his faith, despite the testimony and pretentious sophistries and wit of ten thousand infidels. God has opened your eyes. Satan has blinded theirs. Your testimony is positive. Theirs is negative, and necessarily worthless. A lawyer told his client that two men would swear that they had seen him commit the murder. "Ah, but," said he, "I can bring fifty men who will swear that they didn't see me commit it!" And that poor villain, guilty, but merry with his

[1] Psalm xix. 1. [2] Psalm xxxiv. 8.

own stupid conceit, is a fair type of infidelity It can bring men, in great numbers, it must be owned, who will swear right lustily, and with no little cursing, that they never saw any beauty or glory in Christ or His gospel. And when they have wrapped this, their whole testimony, in the mists of an unintelligible philosophy, and played off the machinery of an historical criticism, which can prove with equal ease, and by the same process,[1] that neither Jesus nor Bonaparte ever lived, so that man has had no Redemption and the French no Revolution, and have then joined in a loud laugh at the deluded "saints" who still prefer Paul to Mr. Hume, John to Mr. Newman, and Jesus Christ to Dr. Strauss, then infidelity has but one thing more which it can do,—change its voice, put on a new disguise, and begin again.

If these men be followed, they will be found to be blind leaders of the blind, and both will fall into the ditch.[2]

[1] As Archbishop Whately has shown in his "Historic Doubts," etc.

[2] Mat., xv. 14.

II.—HIS POVERTY.

See now a sad result of this blindness,—deep poverty. In this too is Bartimeus an image of every unregenerate soul. Both are poor.

When may a man be called poor? Is wealth for the body alone? Has the heart no riches? May not a mind be impoverished, a soul be bankrupt? Ah! yes, there are riches besides money, wealth to which gold and rubies are as nothing.[1]

A man is poor when his need is not supplied. The higher the wants, the deeper the kind of poverty; the more the wants, the deeper its degree. A man with neither food nor shelter, is poorer than he who lacks shelter only. And is not the man without love or hope, poorer than he who has merely no fire nor bread? Who shall deny the name of poor to him whose *soul* is unfurnished? What is the chaff to the wheat,[2] the body to the soul? Are not the soul's desires larger and

[1] James, ii. 5; Prov., viii. 10, 11; Job, xxviii. 12–19.
[2] Jer., xxiii. 28.

more insatiable than those of the flesh? Does not the heart hunger? Is there no such thing as "a famine of truth and love?" Do desolate spirits never cower and shiver and freeze, like houseless wretches in stormy winter nights? Night and winter and storm—are they not also for the soul? And when it has no home in its desolations, no refuge from its foes, no shelter from the blast, no food for its hunger, no consolation in its sorrows, is it not poor? poor in the deepest poverty, which almost alone deserves the name of poverty?[1]

How much of such poverty is there, dwelling in princely halls, clothed in purple and fine linen, and faring sumptuously every day! How often does it walk in royal processions, and flash with jewels, and handle uncounted gold! How much in the circles of wealthy "fashionable life," as it is called, by which weak souls are so dazzled, and for which weak breasts so ache! Fashionable life—with its suspicion and envy and falsehood; its little

[1] "That man only is poor in this world, who lives without Jesus; and that man only is rich with whom Jesus delights to dwell."—THOMAS A KEMPIS.

meannesses and splendid cheats; its magnificent desolations and gorgeous misery! There is poverty indeed.

But let me not forget. It may also be sober and industrious and plain, and have its pew in orthodox churches. I see it before me. It has its likeness in Bartimeus, but its dreadful reality, O sinner, in you!

I saw a man beginning a long journey. It was a most perilous journey, through a wild, inhospitable country. It did not seem so at first; a green and flowery lane led from his dwelling. The road was smooth, the day bright, friends near, the prospect fair. He set gaily off in an easy carriage, attended by assiduous servants, and followed by wagons loaded with all curious provision for present amusement or need. Song and fragrance filled the morning air, and though as the early hours flew by, these fled with them, still his spirits were high, and the wheels rattled merrily over the graded way. The smiles and congratulations of friends saluted him as he passed, and some envied him. He counted himself happy, and rejoicing in his admirable appointments, gave up his heart to pleasure. The evening of the first day has come, and lo! the carriage is going down a hill. How steep it is getting! Faster and faster it goes. The air darkens, the gloom thickens, it grows cold; and faster, faster rolls the carriage downward. Nothing can check it. He tries, the servants try. He shrieks for help, but in vain. Downward dash the horses. And see! at the bottom of the hill, a river, dark and without a bridge. The road leads into it. In rush the horses, and with struggles and groans and plunges of agony, all disappears.

But our traveler did not die in the stream. At the other shore he came forth from the water, cold, desolate, alone. His servants were gone. His treasure was gone. His amusements were gone. And on that bleak shore, in that bitter clime, bound still for that awful journey, I saw him standing, pale, weak, in helpless despair. On, on he must go. He was hungry, but he had no food; thirsty, but there was no water; foot-sore, but he must walk. See, he totters, but he has no staff; dangers assail him, but he has no defence; remorse gnaws him, but he has now no resource. An irresistible destiny urges him, and while the hunger ever bites, and the way grows rougher, and horrors thicken about him, on, on he must go.

Yet he knew all this from the first, but counted it nothing. All his preparations were for the pleasant road, through green and sunny fields. He seemed rich then. Men called him so, all but one honest soul, who frankly told him that his arrangements were short-sighted, wretched, and that if he went thus, his folly was as egregious as soon his poverty would be dreadful. But he was called a rude man for his pains, and bidden begone. Why should he be ever disturbing the present joy with his doleful prophecies? The very sight of him made one melancholy, and his voice seemed to *toll* out his warning, like a dismal bell at a funeral. "Let us use the joys we have, while we have them, and let the future take care of itself!" So he spoke, and so he went; and now there he is.

Nay, you need not tell me that my picture

is preposterous—that there is no such fool on earth. I know how wise the children of this world are in their generation,[1] and how unnatural all this would be, if I meant the petty concerns of this life alone. But suppose I strip off the veil, and tell you that eternity is that awful journey, and life that pleasant lane, and the body that easy carriage in which the soul sets out so gaily, and death that bridgeless river, where friends can go no further, and servants must forsake us, and all the treasure of earth go down for ever? Where *now* is the unnaturalness? Has it not become natural enough—tame even, from its very commonness? Thus from your own mouth I condemn you, and from the shock you feel, when the whole scene is bounded by an inch of time, convict you of unutterable madness in preparing for the little course of this life only, and going all unfurnished for everlasting ages.

As I bid you then, in God's name, beware, shall I be driven away as too rough for your polite ears and tender nerves? Shall I fear

[1] Luke, xvi. 8.

lest I describe the coming terrors of your remorse and shame and utter desolation, of your fiery, unappeasable thirst, and eternal deep poverty, so graphically, that you shall be really alarmed, and set to securing the true riches? Must I measure my periods, and make mild words drop trippingly from my tongue, lest you should believe me to be in earnest?

O souls, let me deal truly by God's Word, and by you. Let me tell you that you *are* poor, miserably poor, and in danger of eternal poverty. Poor? You have no Almighty Comforter for your sorrows,[1] no Infinite Redeemer for your sins,[2] no Eternal God for your portion.[3] You have no solid peace in this world,[4] no well-grounded hope for another,[5] no security for one moment more out of hell.[6] You are an alien from God's people, a stranger from his covenants of promise.[7] You are without the only blood which can pardon,[8] the only Spirit who can pu-

[1] John, xiv. 17. [2] Acts, iv. 12. [3] Mat., xxiv. 51.
[4] Isa., xlviii. 22. [5] Job, xi. 20; Prov., xi. 7.
[6] Mat., xii. 19, 20. [7] Eph., ii. 12. [8] John, iii. 18.

rify,[1] the only righteousness which can justify,[2] without title to heaven,[3] without meetness for it,[4] without any hope of it, except a hope which is false and shall fail you in the day of need.[5] Ah, "you are without Christ and have no God,"[6] and that is poverty indeed, unspeakable, intolerable!

Bartimeus' blindness caused his poverty; and your blindness, that is, your sin, has caused yours. His blind eyes could not see all his poverty, and your blind souls cannot see yours. He could get rid of poverty, only by getting rid of blindness; and it is only by getting rid of sin, that you shall escape being everlastingly poor.

III.—HIS BEGGARY.

See now to what a sad strait this blind man's malady has brought him—he is a *beggar*. Blindness has made him poor, and poverty a beggar. In this, too, he shows the woful estate of the sinner. Every sinner is a

[1] John, iii. 5, 6. [2] Job, xxv. 4; Rom., iii. 19–26.
[3] Rev., xxii. 14, 15. [4] Heb., xii. 14. [5] Mat., vii. 21, 26, 27
[6] Eph., ii. 12.

beggar. How can it be otherwise? Can such poverty be independent? In outward poverty, a well-furnished mind, a wealthy soul may be an inward solace. But when it is the soul that is bankrupt, there is no region still within, where it may retire and comfort itself. It *will* seek for happiness, and it *must* look without—it is forced to beg.

You have seen a blind beggar in your streets. He stands at the corner where the crowd hurries by. He hears the confused hum of busy life—the cries of the drivers, the earnest voices of men, the merry laugh of children. How lively and happy they all seem to him in his melancholy darkness; all happier than he, the poor blind beggar! In one hand he holds his long staff, while the other is reaching forth for alms. His form is bent with weariness and age. He often stands with his head uncovered, through a deference which befits his lowly errand; and then you may see that his hair is thin and white. His meek face and lips moving, but saying nothing, his outstretched hand and sightless eyes turning this way and that, as if they tried to see and could not—these touch the heart and plead for him as no words could do.

And thus I see poor, guilty, blinded souls begging—begging of earth and sky and air and sea, of every passing event, of one another, of all but the great and merciful God, who would supply all their need through Jesus Christ.[1] They must beg. The vast desires of the soul, which God gave that they might be filled from Himself, and which nothing but His own fulness can satisfy; the noble powers degraded to work with trifles; the aspirations which thrill only as they mount heavenward, but now struggle and pant like an eagle with broken wing and his breast in the dust; the deathless conscience, filled with guilt and touched with unappeasable wrath, drugged, indeed, and often sleeping heavily, but waking surely, and then lashing the soul inexorably—all these compel it to be a beggar. They constrain it to cry out, with the lost fiend,

> "Me, miserable! which way shall I fly?"

It is not yet conscious, indeed, of a "hell"

[1] Philippians, iv. 19.

within, but its elements are there, and the uneasy burning keeps it for ever restless.

The soul was made for good, and for good it will ever cry. However debased and fallen, it still hungers for good. It may be a diseased hunger now; but it is not less ravenous for that. If it cannot find food, it will devour offal.

In its ruin, the soul feels itself an exile and vagabond. It is like a prince stolen away from his home in early childhood, and ever retaining some dim remembrance of the glory of his ancient heritage. Amid its deep poverty the royal instinct sometimes stirs within it, and it wanders weeping through the world, in search of that Eden which is no longer on earth.

"Poor pensioner on the bounties of an hour,"

the impoverished soul looks for each new hour to bring some good it has not yet. Disappointed each night, it wakes each day to beg anew its daily bread. "Who will show me any good?"[1] is its constant cry, and hither and

[1] Psalm iv. 6.

thither, to and fro over the face of the earth, it wanders, searching evermore for the satisfaction which still it finds not.

Begging begins in childhood. We beg then with eager hope. We are sure we shall not be disappointed. Games, holidays, sight-seeing all promise much, and childhood begs them to make it blessed. Vexed, wearied, sent empty away again and again, the boy sees, further on, the youth, pursuing his greater hopes, and hastens to join him, confident that in higher excitements and larger liberty, in new aspirations and tenderer love, his soul's thirst shall be slaked. Deluded once more, he grows sober and wise and firm. He is older. He is a man. He lays deep plans now, puts on a bolder face, and begs with sterner importunity. He can take no denial. He *must* have happiness; he *will* be blessed. Fame, wealth, power—these have the hidden treasure he has sought so long. He knows now where it is, and they must give it up. Years are passing, his time will soon be gone, and now he begs indeed! How these idols lead his soul captive! How he toils, cringes, grovels, sacrifices for their favor. Fame, wealth, power—deceitful gods! still promise that to-morrow the long-sought good shall be given. But how many to-morrows come and go, and leave him still trusting to the next! Now he forsakes the pleasures he might have, dries up the fountains of his early love, sweeps all sentiment from his heart, crushes his dearest affections, tasks every power to the utmost, wrings out his heart's blood, and lays all his soul before his idol's feet,—and is disappointed! Disappointed alike in failure and success! If he wins the prize, *this* is not what he coveted, and worshipped, and bargained away his soul for, and he curses it for a cheat. If he fails, he still believes that the true good *was* there, and he was near it; and he curses the chance or envy or hate which snatched it from his grasp.

But who shall describe the *base arts* of this beggary? The disguises, the pretences, the fawnings — all the low tricks of street-beggars — are adopted and eclipsed by those who *will* be rich, will be great, will have fame.

And what are *the profits* of thus begging the world for what God alone can give?

Observe a street-beggar for awhile. How many go by and give nothing, where one drops even a penny in the hat! So many of the passing things of time refuse altogether to give the soul the good it asks.

See again. Do you mark the impudent leer of that mean boy? He knows the beggar is blind, and so he comes up pretending sympathy, and puts a pebble, a chip, in that trembling hand. So a thousand times have you seen the world do for a begging soul.

But there comes a still meaner boy; *he* puts that which, when the grateful old man's hand closes on it pierces or stings it, and, laughing loudly in the blind, bewildered face, he runs away. And thus have I seen the gay, polished world put a sparkling cup to the young man's lips; but when at last it bit him like a serpent and stung him like an adder, the polished world jeered his imprudence, and turned him from its door. His excesses and agony and death must not be seen there!

And when the beggar's gains for the day are

fairly counted, what are they? A few copper coins, foul with gangrene, and little bits of silver, rarely,—enough to buy a scanty meal and a poor lodging, and to-morrow all is to begin again. And thus the world gives—few pleasures, low pleasures, brief pleasures. They stay the soul's hunger for awhile, but never satisfy it, so that straightway we must go out and beg again. The world never raised a man's soul above beggary. It is both too selfish and too poor. It gives but little of what it has, and if it gave all, gave itself, *that* would not fill and bless an immortal soul.

These things make me think how sadly all this begging from the world ends. The hour comes when the world can do no more. It is a bitter hour—an hour of pain and anguish, of weakness and despair—the hour of death. The world is roaring away as ever, in business and mirth, all unconscious that the poor man who loved and worshipped it so, is dying. His banqueting halls, where the world used to riot, are shut. A strange guest came in, unasked, and few cared to stay with him. The revelry hushed, the splendor grew dark. He took the host by the hand, astonished and speechless, and led him to his chamber, and laid him on the bed, and whether others slept or waked, *he* was a constant watcher—with those cold, sleepless eyes! Not many may cross the threshold now, and they tread lightly, and speak in whispers. Even the blessed light of day may no more come in freely at the windows. The gloom and solitude and dreadful stillness of the grave are already closing round him. His pillow smoothed again, another drop of water, and the chill dews of the everlasting night wiped once more from his brow—this is all the poor man has to ask from the world. It is all the world has to give.

But oh, the begging of God which now begins! Bitter crying to Him whose gracious heart has been waiting to bless these many years,[1] waiting in vain for one sigh of contrition, one prayer of faith to His infinite grace! But it is too late. His patient, insulted Spirit has been grieved at length.[2] He has departed. In anger He hath shut up His tender mercies.

[1] Mat., xxiii. 37. [2] Eph., iv. 30.

He will be favorable no more. His mercy is clean gone for ever.[1] He gives no answer, and the soul, beggared now eternally, goes into outer darkness,[2] and begins its blind, everlasting wanderings in the land of blackness and emptiness!

[1] Ps. lxxvii. 7–9.

[2] Mat., xxv. 30

II.

"And hearing the multitude pass by, he asked what it meant, and they told him that Jesus of Nazareth passeth by."

BLINDNESS, poverty, beggary! What woes to be mingled in one cup! Who can measure the wretchedness of the man who is ever drinking their still unexhausted bitterness? Let us pity Bartimeus. But do not forget the deeper sorrows of which these were but the shadow. I see more miserable souls before me. I can weep over Bartimeus, but when I look at many of you, I am amazed that I ever cease to weep. What hardness has seized my heart that I can think of you without tears, or meet you without lamentation? The heavens are astonished at your wretchedness and doom, and why doth not horror take hold on my soul?[1] Oh that my head were waters, and mine eyes a foun-

[1] Jer., ii. 12, 13; Ps. cxix. 53.

tain of tears, that I might weep day and night for you,[1] O ye blinder blind, and poorer poor than Bartimeus!

Ah! if it were only the eye of the body that is out! only the flesh that is clothed with rags! Yet that would be dreadful. It *was* dreadful in visions of the night, when deep sleep falleth on men.[2] Then I dreamed that Sabbath morning had come, and I stood in my pulpit to preach; when suddenly I saw paleness gathering on all faces; for God was wrapping you in His cloud and thick darkness, and I stood alone among a congregation of the blind. Then a change passed over your bright raiment, and it became rags—the coarse rags of beggars. All bloom fled from every cheek, and every form was shrivelled and bent. A horrible old age had come even on the faces of little children. Ah! what a scene it was! Some of you groped your fearful way in the dark. Some shrieked in frenzy. Some stretched your bony hands and turned your hunger-bitten faces toward heaven, and with eyes that wept their own blindness, cried in

[1] Jer., ix. 1. [2] Job, iv. 13.

anguish for light; while some sat still, petrified with horror. Yet I knew you all as before. I looked down on the same dear faces, wretched now, and ghastly, the same gentle eyes through which loving souls had so often looked in kindness on me,—now distorted and wild, and "rolling in vain to find the day."

When grief and astonishment would let me, I tried to speak, but none heard me. I called aloud; but screams and sobs and deep-drawn sighs, and curses muttered through gnashing teeth, drowned my voice. When lo! amid the great bitterness and struggle of my soul, I heard the voice of God saying unto me, "Weep not, nor be dismayed for this; but weep for souls that see not, and hearts that are blind. Weep for the desolations of sin, of which I have now shown thee a little, lest I visit the people in mine anger, and there be no remedy; lest I smite them in my wrath, and their blindness be everlasting. Weep for them."

The awful voice had made a great silence, and now again it spoke, and said to you, with a benignant sweetness which melted your hearts and poured sunbeams on your darkness, "O ye wretched, and miserable, and poor, and blind, and naked; I counsel you to buy of me gold tried in the fire, that ye may be rich; and white raiment that ye may be clothed, and that the shame of your nakedness do not appear; and anoint your eyes with eye-salve that ye may see!"[1]

Will you not weep for yourselves, ye blind souls? Will you not believe God's testimony declaring your ruin and proclaiming a remedy? Will you not taste and see that the Lord is gracious?[2] Will you not follow on to know the Lord[3] as He reveals His loving-kindness, in this story, in which human misery and divine mercy so strangely meet, and mercy so blessedly triumphs? Consent to begin in the depths with Bartimeus, and one day you shall stand on the heights with him, praising his God and yours with irrepressible rejoicing.

But, poor man! his song is not yet. He still sits by the high-way, as unconscious as the dead, of the blessing which even now slowly draws near, and soon shall pour around

[1] Rev., iii. 18. [2] Psalm xxxiv. 8. [3] Hosea, vi. 3.

and through him its streams of earthly and heavenly light.

There he sits in his dreary darkness, while from the Throne an Eye of pity is looking down upon him, and from the gates of heaven loving angels are pouring forth,[1] to behold a new triumph of the power and grace of their Lord,[2] and welcome a new companion to their everlasting joy,[3] and that Lord Himself is coming nearer, nearer, with his heart yearning for its gracious overflow. That celestial virtue, which dwelt in unmeasured fulness in Him and poured out so freely that, if faith's finger touched even the hem of His garment, its liberal streams emptied themselves till all human need was filled,[4]—that virtue was even now springing up from the deep wells of His Deity and thrilling His human heart with secret joy.

And is it not always so? Does not God always begin with man? What has man, except his miseries, to attract any thing in God? And what can these attract but grace—pure

[1] Heb., i. 14. [2] 1 Peter, i. 12.
[3] Luke, xv. 10. [4] Luke, viii. 43–48.

grace coming in place of deserved wrath? And when even this comes, it finds no welcome or congenial home. "The grace of God in the heart of man," says Leighton, "is a tender plant in a strange, unkindly soil." Both the seed and the sunshine, then, must come from heaven. To him that hath, indeed, shall be given,[1] but then what have we that we did not receive?[2] *Every* good gift is from above.[3] Have we repentance? Him hath God exalted with His right hand to be a Prince and Saviour, for to *give repentance* to Israel, and forgiveness of sins.[4] Pardon is no more the gift of Christ than the repentance that leads to it. Have we faith? It is the gift of God.[5] Jesus is its Author as well as Finisher.[6] Have we love? We love Him because He first loved us.[7] Love, joy, peace, long-suffering, gentleness, goodness, faith, meekness, temperance, are all the *fruit* of the Spirit;[8] while if you would see what fruit springs of itself from the vine of nature, you may read just before,[9] where Paul counts over

[1] Luke, xix. 26. [2] 1 Cor., iv. 7. [3] James, i. 17.
[4] Acts, v. 31. [5] Eph., ii. 8. [6] Heb., xii. 2.
[7] 1 John, iv. 19. [8] Gal., v. 22, 23. [9] Gal., v. 19–21.

seventeen bitter, deadly clusters, and then, weary of the dreadful count, adds, "and such like." When God begins to deal graciously with us, passing by us in pity, and looking on us in love, to make us His in everlasting espousals, we are described under the image of a miserable infant, born in an accursed land and of accursed parents, and cast out immediately, unpitied, into the open field, exposed, helpless, bleeding, polluted, to die![1] And in many other Scriptures we are declared to be by nature, dead in trespasses and sins, lying in wickedness, children of wrath, having minds which are enmity against God, of our father the devil.[2] And if the likeness, corruption and curse of hell are not ours for ever, the change from first to last is of God. "Men find a thing lovely, and love it; God loves a thing, and thereby makes it lovely."[3]

In this case, it is indeed brought to pass that the first word shall come from Bartimeus. But Christ, who is coming near on purpose to bless him, has, by His Providence, arranged

[1] Ezek. xvi. [2] Eph., ii. 1; 1 John, v. 19; Eph., ii. 3; Rom., viii. 7; John, viii. 44. [3] Jenkyn on Jude.

it that he shall be sitting there as He is to pass by, that he should have some previous knowledge of Jesus of Nazareth and His power to heal, that his curiosity shall be awakened and his desires excited, while through His grace alone, he has faith to call Him Lord and trust his cure to His power and compassion.[1]

There he sits hoping for mere worldly gain. He has not come to meet Christ. It was not in all his thoughts to get his eyes opened.

How many like him are before me,—dying sinners on whom God's curse is resting, who yet did not come to secure the great salvation. You have gathered in the place of mercy, but not as fugitives from the wrath that is pursuing you. You knew that Christ was preached here in every sermon, but you did not come to meet Him. How many of this perishing multitude came for no higher reason than that others were coming, and you knew not well what else to be doing meantime, or you thought it decent to come, or you like to hear sermons. For these and such reasons you have dared to seat yourselves in the house of God, and come

[1] Cor., xii. 3; Eph., ii. 8.

under the tremendous responsibilities of hearers of the gospel! To stroll through sacred places, careless spectators of the crucifixion; indifferent lookers-on while God comes down in tempest and blackness on Mt. Sinai, to give His dreadful Law!

God grant a further parallel; that you may get what you did not come for, even a solemn meeting and saving closing of your souls with Jesus Christ.

There sits the blind man, when a faint sound catches his quick ear. He listens, and perceives a noise of many foot-steps, a murmur of many voices, confused and distant. On they come, and hope rises high in his breast. To-day shall be a harvest to him. It is rare that so many pass at once, and now will he be diligent. On they come, and louder grows the sound of steps, the swell of voices. Wonder mingles with his hope,—wonder what all this means, for now they are near, and plainly it is a great multitude.

A multitude with Jesus! a multitude of followers! How can he then complain, I have labored in vain, I have spent my strength for naught?[1] Simply because He had many followers, but few friends; many from curiosity, many for loaves, many for fashion, but few from faith, few from love. And so it has been ever since.

A multitude with Jesus! But it is not all following that blesses. Judas followed Him daily, but remained to the end the thief and devil he was from the beginning.[2] Once the people not only followed but thronged Him; but only one was healed, and she touched but the hem of His garment. They pressed upon Him, but hers was the only touch of faith.[3] Mere outward connection with Christ did no man any good. And so it has been ever since.

A multitude with Jesus! Yes, when His march is at all triumphal,—when as He goes He invests His progress with the splendor of miracles, there will be no want of a crowd to gape after Him. But though He fed as well as dazzled them yesterday, a little hard doctrine preached to-day thins them with a wit-

[1] Isa., xlix. 4. [2] John, vi. 70; Mat., xxvi. 24; xxvii. 5
[3] Mark, v. 27, 31, 34.

ness. No man, said Jesus, can come unto me, except it were given unto him of my Father. From that time many of His disciples went back and walked no more with Him.[1] And so it has been ever since.

A multitude with Jesus! Take care, then, ye members of the church. Examine yourselves closely. Profession of religion is easy now. Numbers give power, respectability, fashion, even enthusiasm. See! They spread their costly raiment in His path. They pave His way with purple. The thunder of their hosannahs goes up to heaven.[2] But to-morrow He is alone, and the multitude grow hoarse with hooting and cursing Him.[3] So little was the applause of the multitude worth; so little did popularity test principle in the days of Jesus. And so it has been ever since.

A multitude with Jesus! Blessed be God, *in* that multitude some true disciples may be found; some who, though weak and sinning,—forward, like Peter, when they should be backward,[4] and then backward, of course, when

[1] John, vi. 65, 66.
[2] Mat., xxi. 8, 9.
[3] Luke, xxiii. 18, 21, 23.
[4] Mat., xvi. 22.

they should be forward;[1] ambitious, like Zebedee's children,[2] or doubting like Thomas,[3] are still true friends of Jesus, living for Him, suffering for Him, growing like Him day by day, and dying for Him without a murmur, if He so appoint. Always remember that. Jesus Christ has never been left without true followers. Among the professed people of God there have always been real people of God. So it was in the days of Christ. And so it has been ever since.

"And *hearing* the multitude." O what a blessing is that! His ears are open though his eyes are shut. Thus God remembers to be gracious. Where He takes one mercy He leaves another. He never takes all until the cup of iniquity is full,[4] and then wrath comes to the uttermost and shivers it.[5] He leaves even the heathen without excuse, for they may know His eternal power and Godhead from the works of creation.[6] And no sinner need flatter himself that because the Bible calls him blind or dead, he shall therefore

[1] Mat., xxvi. 58. [2] Mat., xx. 20–24. [3] John, xx. 25.
[4] Gen., xv. 16. [5] 1 Thes., ii. 16. [6] Rom., i. 20, 32; ii. 14, 15.

escape duty or condemnation. The same epistle which pronounces sinners dead in trespasses and sins, shouts in their ears, Awake, thou that sleepest, and arise from the dead and Christ shall give thee light![1]

Yes sinners, you are blind; you cannot see spiritual beauty or glory. But you can 'hear' of them, and know that you must see them or perish.

"But *I* cannot open my eyes. So you have told me again and again. You say I am helpless."

You are indeed; but it remains nevertheless true that you must see or perish.

"Is not this a hard case? Is not such preaching mockery? I *cannot* open my eyes."

True, true, and the more's the pity. It *is* a hard case. For the constitution of heaven will not be changed by your helplessness. Christ tells us that none are blessed but they who see God, and that only the pure in heart shall see Him.[2] But your heart is foul with sin which God hates, and its foulness has

[1] Eph., ii. 1 v. 14. [2] Mat., v. 8.

blinded your eyes and brought you under His curse. So that you are, indeed, in helpless blindness. And yet you must see or perish.

"But why preach this to me? If I am helpless why urge me with impossible duties and vain responsibilities?"

Because it is true that you are helpless, and true that you must see or perish. Both are awful truths of God's word, and it greatly concerns you to know them. I see indeed that you would silence me by this logic. You think that in pleading your inability, you have an argument that will excuse you from the duties you hate. Very well; suppose you do silence me. God will still call to you, Repent or perish,[1] Believe or be damned![2] And if you do excuse yourself from these hateful duties, do you know that you will also excuse yourself from salvation? You need not see, you need not believe. God will not compel your vision or your faith. But He *will* compel you to believe or be damned, to see or be lost. So all your logic has done for

[1] Luke, xiii. 3, 5. [2] Mark, xvi. 16.

you is to shut you out of heaven. But perhaps you do not *believe* that you are helpless. Then prove your power by opening your eyes. Try it. *See*, if you can. Look around on the regions of spiritual beauty. Delight yourself with the saints' blessedness. God's light and love are pouring all around you, and they will pour into you, if you can but open your eyes. . . . There, have you done it? Do they fill you with light? Bathe your soul with wonder and bliss? Ah! have you failed? Are you still blind? Is all dark? Is your heart still cold and hard? Alas, then you *are* helpless, and may *never* see! Yet if you do not see you must perish!

"Ah, me! what then shall I do?"

What! are you indeed convinced that you have no power to open your eyes? And yet that you must see or perish?

"Yes, alas! I feel my utter helplessness, while the Law of God is urging me with its heavy requirements. I know I can have no heaven but in the vision of God reconciled, and smiling on me. O that would indeed be heaven! But I do not, cannot see Him. I am blind, and can do nothing. O wretched man that I am, who shall deliver me?"[1]

Now, sinner, you find the use of preaching your helplessness and your duty together. The merciless dilemma has met you at either hand, and shut you up to the faith of the gospel.[2] You have learned to despair of your own strength, and cry out for a deliverer. Then you were in no haste to obey God, for what you could do at any time, why should you not choose your own time for? You would wait for a convenient season. But now that shield of vain confidence is cast away, and your naked heart bared to every arrow from the quiver of God. You lie helpless before a Sovereign God, justly condemned, and hopelessly lost, unless He save you. And *now* I may tell you what to do.

Do what Bartimeus did. Hear the truth, bear the truth, believe the truth. Settle it for ever in your heart that if you do not see your infinite need of a Saviour, and Christ's infinite fitness to be your Saviour, you are lost. Then cry to Jesus Christ to open your eyes. Salva-

1 Rom., vii. 24. 2 Gal., iii. 23.

tion is by faith,[1] and faith is by hearing,[2] and you have hearing, you do hear—hear that you are blind, and the wrath of God is on you,[3] and the vengeance of hell awaits you,[4] and none but Jesus Christ can save you,[5] and He can![6] You hear that, and I pray you make speedy use of it, or *that* will be taken away, with every other sense and power, and this death in sin will deepen into death in hell—death in blindness and despair for ever!

I have seen Laura Bridgman, whom God sent into this world without sight, hearing, or the power of speech. She could see nothing, hear nothing, ask nothing. To her the very thunder has ever been silence, and the sun blackness. The tips of her fingers and the palms of her hands have been her eyes and ears and tongue. Yet that poor sickly girl knows much of the earth and language and numbers; of human relationships and passions; of what is, has been, shall be, should be; of sin and death and hell; of God and Christ and Heaven. And all this has gone

[1] Eph., ii. 8. [2] Rom., x. 17. [3] John, iii. 36.
[4] Mat., xxv. 41. [5] Acts, iv. 12. [6] 1 Tim., i. 15.

through the poor child's slender fingers, darkly feeling the fingers of another; and thus she tells her hopes and fears and sorrows. And if she, groping so blindly for the Saviour, finds Him, and rests her weak hands on His lowly Head,—that blessed Head which bows lowly enough even for this,—O how will she rise up in judgment,[1] and condemn, with utter overwhelming, you, oh, sinners, upon whose souls every sense is pouring the knowledge of God, while your eyes read His Holy Word, and your ears hear, a thousand times over, these tidings of great joy,—even the glorious gospel of the blessed God![2]

"Hearing the multitude pass by, he asked what it meant." So this inarticulate preaching of the passing multitude arrested the attention of the blind man, and awakened his curiosity, and set him to inquiring the meaning of these things. "Hearing, he asked." Yes, yes, that is the true progression. If there is a movement in the church, if a new impulse is given to the power of godliness, if Christ walks amidst His people,[3] even though false

[1] Mat., xii. 41, 42. [2] 1 Tim. i. 11 [3] Rev., ii. 1.

professors gather with them; if the tread of Zion on the earth is like the tread of an army with banners,[1] then will a blind, ungodly world be arrested from its hungry, clamorous quest after mere earthly gain. It will consider and wonder and inquire. If the church, —if you, my brethren, will cease to wander or dance or drudge wherever the world does; if you will be awake and up, and gather nearer to Christ and thus nearer to each other; if you will move *onward* with Christ, then men *will* look up. Old Avarice will drop his muck-rake, and Ambition forget to chase his bubble, and on the highway or byway, in court and camp and on 'change, men will pause and look; and the movements of a spiritual church will make them wonder, and they will inquire, (while no little awe is creeping over their hearts,) What do these things mean? Where are these men going? Why do they seem like strangers and pilgrims, with their loins girded and their faces set toward some far-off country?[2] Why are they so earnest? Why do they seem to walk above

[1] Song, vi. 10. [2] Heb., xi. 13; Luke, xii. 35; Jer., l. 5.

above the world,[1] while yet they scatter ten thousand sweet charities as they pass? What means their strange speech like an unearthly harmony? Why do they sing in the way, brave songs of glory, even when the cloud wraps them, and the driving storm beats them with its hail?

If Zion thus moved on with her King in the midst of her,[3] how would the thunder of her triumph shake the earth! Ah, brethren, if you, just you, thus moved on under the Captain of your salvation, how would this city be stirred! Your life would then be preaching all over the town,—in every street and lane, and it would be preaching which would crowd this house continually with anxious inquirers. In my heart I believe it; every seat and standing-place would be filled, and the place be speedily too strait for us,[4] and that cheering cry be heard again among us, Let us rise up and build.[5] Then would these courts be still and awful. Believers would find it hard to be absent. Pious affections, deep

[1] Prov., xv. 24. [2] Ps. cxxxviii. 5. [3] Zech., iii. 15, 17.
[4] Isa., xlix. 20. [5] Neh., ii. 18.

adorations, importunate desires would fill their hearts and go up to heaven. With what power would they sing! With what fervor would they pray! With what holy relish would they eat the simple food of the gospel! And how would the unpardoned hang with painful anxiety on the words of life! How simple and easy would preaching then be,—yet savoring so preciously of life everlasting through Christ crucified.

Shall I describe a sermon which would refresh the people of God, and be as arrows in the hearts of His enemies,[1] till they became willing captives of Christ?[2]

My text shall be my guide. The road-side was the church, the multitude preached, and Bartimeus was the hearer. And now for the sermon;—"And they told him, Jesus of Nazareth passeth by." "Jesus of Nazareth passeth by!" That is the whole of it, and I think it a very good one, when we consider the occasion. At any rate it enchained the whole mind and heart of Bartimeus. It went down into his soul like a beam of light, and filled him with

[1] Psalm xlv. 5. [2] Psalm cx. 3.

amazement and joy. It was the strangest, gladdest word he had ever heard. 'Jesus of Nazareth—the Saviour—He who openeth the eyes of the blind! Is He here—so near me—where I may speak to Him? O has the day come at last, when my eyes shall be opened? When I shall see, shall see, and be no more a beggar? O can such news be true?'

So you see it was a *powerful* sermon. It went to the heart and took complete possession of it. I am quite sure Bartimeus was not a captious critic of *that* sermon. He had no time to think whether it was uttered fast or slowly, loudly or gently. But what made it so powerful? "Jesus of Nazareth passeth by." That is all of it. I am afraid many of us would think very little of such a sermon. But Bartimeus felt his blindness and his need of Christ. There is the difference. The power of the sermon was in the state of the hearer's heart. A sermon often seems poor because we are cold. There is a difference in sermons, no doubt. But I read that men could go to sleep while Paul preached,[1] and even the wise

[1] Acts, xx. 9.

men of Athens called him a babbler and mocked,[1] while the most noble Festus, who was a gentleman in high life, and should have known better, interrupted him in the midst of his sermon, and pronounced him "mad,"[2]—crazy, as we would say. If sinners and saints felt their needs more,—if they oftener came from secret devotions, the simplest things we could say of Christ would be like bread to the hungry and cold waters to the thirsty soul.[3]

It was a very *simple* sermon. Who cannot preach it? "Jesus of Nazareth passeth by." There is no follower of Jesus who cannot tell poor blind souls this. Yet this is the message which is to save the world. The Bible tells it over in a thousand forms. Fill your hearts with them, and go, tell the glad tidings to lost sinners every where. I thank God that the gospel is so simple that the whole multitude of Christ's followers can preach it.

And so must the preaching from the pulpit be simple. We must say many things that our hearers already know. A good preacher tries to make all truth simple. He is a bad

[1] Acts, xvii. 18, 32. [2] Acts, xxvi. 24. [3] Prov., xxv. 25.

shepherd, say the old writers, who holds the hay too high for the sheep. According to Lord Bacon, little minds love to inflate plain things into marvels, while great minds love to reduce marvels to plain things.

"The very essence of truth," says Milton, "is plainness and brightness; the darkness and crookedness are our own."[1] "Better the grammarian should reprehend," says Jenkyn, "than the people not understand. Pithy plainness is the beauty of preaching. What good doth a golden key that opens not?"[2] An old lady once walked a great way to hear the celebrated Adam Clarke preach. She had heard he was "such a scholar," as indeed he was. But she was bitterly disappointed, "because," said she, "I understood every thing he said." And I knew a man who left the church one morning quite indignant, because the preacher had one thing in his sermon he knew before! It was a little explanation meant for the children,—dear little things,—they are always coming on, and I love to see their bright little

[1] Reformation in England. Book First.

[2] Exposition upon Jude.

faces among the older people. *We* used to need and prize these simple explanations, and why shouldn't they have them in their turn? And this blessed thing is to be said of the gospel: Let it be made ever so simple, so that little children are drinking it in with grateful wonder, it still has depths and riches to satisfy the mind and heart of the mightiest philosopher, if only he has that highest attainment of wisdom,—a simple, child-like faith. Like the sun, it is mirrored at the same moment by the dew-drop and the ocean.

But best of all, this sermon was *about Christ.* He is mentioned alone. When Bartimeus asked "what it meant," these preachers did not answer, "We are passing by." Yet their movements arrested him; he heard *them.* But when he asked what the multitude meant, they told him "Jesus of Nazareth passeth by." It is a happy thing when the church can say of all its great movements and excitements, "Jesus is passing by." This is a test of revivals, a test of all right Christian effort,— "Jesus passeth by." This is the test too of a good sermon. "The excellency of a sermon," says Flavel, " lies in the plainest discoveries and liveliest applications of Jesus Christ."

They announce that Jesus is near. What blessed tidings to Bartimeus! In this you all agree. It was a great thing for him to have his eyes opened. From these far-off ages your sympathies run back and mingle with his agitation of joy. To have the eyes opened—to see for the first time! The rapture must be indescribable.

And when I announce the nearness of Jesus, now and here, to you, oh sinner, why is not the news joyful? Was it much that those eyes should be opened upon a world darkened by the curse, and stained by the shadow of death, and furrowed so roughly with graves? eyes often to be dimmed with tears and soon with age! eyes whose brief light death should soon quench with the clods of the valley, and leave their hollow sockets to be nests for worms! Yes, yes, I confess it, even this was much. But oh, tell me, in your turn, is it nothing to you that Jesus is again near, and that your eyes may this day be opened to the light of the Cross? light fairer than the moon, clearer than the sun, and making earth radiant with the glories of heaven? light which often streams brightest in death, gilding even the dark valley? light of the everlasting Throne, on which, with saints and angels, you may gaze for ever?

And is it tidings of *this* light alone, which cannot agitate? Is it only eternal salvation that is a trifle? Is it only because the offered blessedness is absolutely immeasurable and everlasting, that it is not worth your thought or care?

Miserable souls! so blind that you do not know your blindness, so blind that you do not believe it, though God declares it, my business now is to tell you that Jesus Christ is near,—He passeth by! Now is your time; make haste to secure your salvation. How near He is! He passeth by in the light of every Sabbath sun, in every Church built to His Name, in every reading of His Word, in every gospel sermon, in sacraments and prayers and psalms, but most of all in every movement of His Spirit on the heart. If you *feel* under the truth, if your conscience confirms what God declares, if you have been made even uneasy in your sin, if like Felix you have trembled,[1] or like Agrippa have been almost persuaded to be a Christian,[2] oh! let me tell you that *I* did not work any of these things in your heart. Who am I, that I can put a pulse in the heart of death?[3] They are not my work, and I dare not claim the glory of them.[4] God's Spirit has been stirring in your heart, striving with you for your eternal salvation! What an awfulness does that give to these services! Jesus, God manifest in the flesh,[5] is here, by His gracious Spirit.[6] He fills every ordinance.[7] He moves from heart to heart. You are in His tremendous presence, under His omniscient eye, in the grasp of His infinite power, in the gracious sphere of His healing love.

But He "passeth *by!*" He will not always tarry.[8] The day of grace is not for ever.[9] Its sun will go down, and the night that follows is eternal despair.[10] Christ never passed that

[1] Acts, xxiv. 25. [2] Acts, xxvi. 28. [3] 2 Kings, v. 6.
[4] Ps. cxv. 1. [5] 1 Tim., iii. 16. [6] John, xvi. 7, 8.
[7] Mat., xviii. 20. [8] John, xii. 35, 36. [9] Gen., vi. 3.
[10] John, viii. 21, 24; Luke, xix. 42.

way again; He may never pass your way again. That was His last visit to Jericho; this call may be His last visit to you. This was Bartimeus' only opportunity; to-day may be your only opportunity.[1] Woe, woe, to Bartimeus, if he lose this golden season! If he does he shall die in his blindness. Woe, a heavier woe to you, O sinner, if you slight this, your golden season, for securing this great salvation![2] This moment may decide your doom. Fly to Jesus Christ!

[1] 2 Cor., vi. 2. [2] Heb., ii. 3.

III.

"And when he heard that it was Jesus of Nazareth, he began to cry out and say, Jesus, thou Son of David, have mercy on me!"

WE left Bartimeus listening to his first gospel sermon. The preachers seem to have done their part well. At any rate their message was good. It was simple, straight-forward and altogether about Jesus Christ.

We do not know *how* they spoke. It would be pleasant, for their sakes, to know that they showed a proper sympathy with the precious words they were saying, and with the poor man who heard them. But if we cannot tell this, we know what concerns us far more,—that they told him the very thing he needed. However rude in speech, they have let him know that the Healer of the blind is near; and I am sure that nothing they could say about any thing else could make up for *not* telling him that. The most eloquent harangue on the politics of the times, though Pilate and Herod and Cæsar, and Roman eagles and Jewish banners, and liberty and nationality and destiny had rolled with splendid imagery through sounding periods, would have been a sad exchange for those simple words,—"Jesus of Nazareth passeth by." Nor would Aristotle's keenest logic, nor Plato's finest speculations have served a whit better. The man was blind, and wanted his eyes opened; and till this was done, these things, however set forth, were but trash and mockery.

Mockery? Are not the preachers of God's Word stewards in Christ's House?[1] And has He not made ready to our hands boundless stores for perishing sinners, and bidden us give as freely as we have received?[2] And when hungry souls come at our call to the gospel feast and wait to be fed, if we give them dry husks of philosophy for the "strong meat" of doctrine, the "stone" of hard metaphysics for the living bread of God's saving truth, and the "scorpion" of envenomed po-

[1] 1 Cor., iv. 1, 2; 1 Pet., iv. 10. [2] Mat., x. 8.

litical fanaticism for the sincere milk of the word, clusters from Eshcol, water from the River of Life, wine of gladness, and manna still wet with the dews with which it came down from heaven,[1]—*is* it not bitterest mockery of the deepest sorrows and basest treachery to the highest trusts?

Nay, if these preachers told their glad tidings in an unfeeling way, it was a great wrong,—a wrong to themselves and Bartimeus and such blessed truth, but still a wrong immeasurably less than *not* to have told such truth, in whatever way.

But if the preacher's responsibility is so dreadful, I pray you, has the hearer no responsibility? If these men tell Bartimeus that Jesus passeth by, though in a way having what faults you please, will he not be the most besotted of fools, if he turns from this glorious opportunity, and gropes his way back to his hovel, to sit down there in poverty and darkness, and sneer or laugh or be angry at these failures in manner or spirit? These

[1] Heb., v. 14; Luke, xi. 11, 12; 1 Pet., ii. 2 Numb., xiii. 23; Rev., xxii. 1; Numb., xi. 9.

things concern them and they must answer for them to God, but what concerns him but that he is blind, and now "Jesus of Nazareth passeth by?"

Take heed, therefore, how ye hear,[1] is the warning of Christ. O there is much in that! If we must take heed to our preaching, you must take heed to your hearing. If an awful account must be given from the pulpit, one hardly less awful must be given from the pew. If it is no light thing to preach the gospel, you will find that it is no light thing to hear the gospel. Eternal salvation depends on right hearing. There are just two kinds of hearing, not three. There is a hearing unto life, and another hearing unto death; but there is no hearing between,—none to indifference. You may try to hear merely that you may hear, and let that be the end of it,—but that will *not* be the end of it. The end of it will be life or death! You may resolve that the preaching shall make no difference in you,—but it will make a difference in you, and the difference will be salvation or perdition! The

[1] Luke, viii. 18.

gospel leaves no man where it found him. If it be not wings to bear him to heaven, it will be a mill-stone to sink him to hell. Some of you think it the lightest of pastimes to come to church and hear a sermon. I warn you that this is a fearful mistake. I will speak to you in the words of God: We are ambassadors for Christ, as though God did beseech you by us: we pray you in Christ's stead, be ye reconciled to God.[1] We are unto God a sweet savor of Christ, in them that are saved and in them that perish: to the one we are the savor of death unto death; and to the other the savor of life unto life.[2] If our gospel be hid, it is hid to them that are lost.[3] This is true always. It is true to-day,—of this sermon. As God is true, this process is now going on in every hearer. Each one of you is this moment fitting either for blessedness with God, or for His wrath in hell; for which, depends on one thing alone,—how you are now hearing. Take heed then, and that you may do this the more intelligently, see further how Bartimeus heard. I think we shall find

[1] 2 Cor., v. 20. [2] 2 Cor., ii. 15, 16. [3] 2 Cor., iv. 3.

most of the marks of a good hearer in him, and I shall notice none other.

I. His hearing *led him to action.* His very soul seemed to be roused, and he began to *do* something.

In contrast with this we see the great fault of gospel hearers in this day. It is not that you are not polite and attentive hearers. Your orderly sitting and solemn listening are even beyond our expectation. When Paul and Stephen and Christ preached, the people often made a tumult. They mocked; they sneered; they cried out and threw dust into the air. They were ready to beat and kill them.[1] You do none of these things. I often wonder you do not. It sometimes makes me fear I have not dealt faithfully with you. Yet I try to preach as plainly as they did. I take their very words, and in the name of God speak them boldly to you. I do not abate one jot of their terrible energy and point. Yea, I take the sword of the Spirit, which is the word of God,[2] and with unsparing hand lay open your hearts. I repeat the tremendous descriptions

[1] John, viii. 59; Acts, xxii. 22, 23, &c., &c. [2] Eph., vi. 17.

which God has given of them; I apply the dreadful names by which He has called you; I sound aloud the threats of His wrath; I strive in every way to make you feel that I am personal,—that I mean you,—every unregenerate soul; and for these things in Christ's day, they would have gnashed on me with their teeth and hurled me out of the city; while you listen so calmly, so complacently, that I cannot tell saint from sinner; the men against whom God's curses are thundered, from those to whom His eternal blessing is sealed; the men, who through sovereign grace are washed, who are sanctified, who are justified in the name of the Lord Jesus, and by the Spirit of our God,[1] from those who are lying in wickedness,[2] the enemies of the cross of Christ,[3] condemned already,[4] and in instant danger of the vengeance of eternal fire![5]

Is it not a marvel? What ails you, O man, that nothing can rouse you—if not to feel right, at least to feel at all? if not to rise and lay hold on eternal life,[6] at least to stir in your

[1] 1 Cor., vi. 11. [2] 1 John, v. 19. [3] Phil., iii. 18.
[4] John, iii. 18. [5] Jude, vii. [6] 1 Tim., vi. 12.

tomb, and give us some token for hope that you are not already past feeling,[1]—blind, deaf, dead, spiritually, utterly, everlastingly dead!

Oh, for a pulse of life in those frozen hearts! A flush of blood, even though it were angry blood, in those pale cheeks! Give me Saul breathing out threatenings and slaughters, rather than Gallio caring for none of these things.[2] Some arrow of truth has pierced the heart of Saul or he would not rage so; and soon you read of him as Paul the Apostle. But I fear Gallio went on in his careless way, till the pains of hell made him care for ever.

"I came to break your head," said a man once to Whitefield, "but by the grace of God you have broken my heart." That was a vile purpose to go to church with, but if he had gone in a complacent frame, and quietly slept or coolly criticised the preacher, it would have been far worse. He would not have carried away that priceless treasure—a broken heart.

If what we say is true, why do you not act upon it? If false, how can you bear to be charged with it? If our charges are false,

[1] Eph., iv. 19. [2] Acts, ix. 1; xviii. 17.

they are also insulting and outrageous. If you *believe* them to be false, your conduct, in hearing them so calmly, and coming back to hear them again, and even sometimes applauding us for the vehement way in which we assail and denounce you, is perfectly astonishing. Why look at it! You gather in a church on a Sabbath morning, and we strip away all your hopes, one by one; we weigh all your moralities and good deeds in the scale of God's law, and, by God's authority, write "wanting" on every one;[1] we cast the light of heaven on your boasted righteousness, and the comely robe, in which you were so confidently wrapped, turns to rags and filthiness;[2] we press on into your very heart, and in God's name, pronounce it deceitful above all things and desperately wicked;[3] and when we have left you thus naked, helpless, guilty and without hope, we show you the storm which death, devils and hell are urging on, and which waits only for the nod of the sin-avenging God whom you have made your enemy, and are now provoking to sweep you as chaff into

[1] Rom., iii. 20. [2] Isa., lxiv. 6. [3] Jer., xvii. 9.

ruin beyond redemption;[1]—and believing all this to be false, you bear it, and go out smiling, and say that was a good sermon, and you like to hear a man preach that way; and that night or the next Sabbath you come back to hear the same things again!

Or if you say you believe these things to be true, your conduct is still more amazing. If true, they should concern you infinitely: yet you are not concerned at all. If true, they are of eternal weight, and should override every business, care and pleasure in the world; yet the lightest trifle of time overrides them, and tramples them in the dust and buries them in utter forgetfulness. You will call Bartimeus a fool if he does not try to get his eyes opened this very day. But what name will you reserve for yourselves, if, while I this day, as one of these ambassadors of God, offer you pardon and healing and eternal life through Jesus Christ, who now passes by to bestow them, you once more refuse the Saviour, and go on as before toward perdition?

[1] Job, xxi. 18.

But Bartimeus is no fool. As he hears he acts. "Jesus of Nazareth passeth by," say the multitude, and straightway the blind eyes fill with tears, the faded cheeks flush with hope, the hands are out-stretched in supplication, and his very soul pours out in the cry, "Jesus, Son of David, have mercy on me!"

II. This reveals to us the second mark of right hearing;—*It fills a man with earnestness.* If he has heard such truth as he ought, he not only acts, but acts with energy. Thus Bartimeus acted. "When he heard he cried out." The word means a great and strong cry. The multitude was around him; but he cared not for that. They were mostly strangers to him; but he cared not for that. Those who did know him knew him as a beggar; but he cared not for that. He had never been in the presence of Christ before; but even this did not deter him. Beggar as he was, he "cried out" before Him, before them all. He felt too deeply the bitterness of blindness, the misery of poverty, the degradation of beggary, to think of these things.

So it must be with you, O sinners. If you

would enter heaven you must be in earnest about it.[1] Men were brought on beds to Christ to be healed,[2] but no man ever went to heaven lying on his bed and borne on the shoulders of others. In the preparations needful for gaining heaven, I find an account of many pieces of hard armor,[3] but no mention of a bed. *There* they rest in their beds,[4] but our rest is not yet. You will never wake up some fine morning and find yourself pious. The great change will not steal softly over you while you sit at ease. You must be awake, and up, and at it. You must strive, says Christ;[5]—Strive like a wrestler who has his foe and his match;—Strive like a runner, when the race is long and the runners many, and but one can win;—Strive as the soldier, when the conflict is sharp, and he who conquers not must die.[6] Such is the Scripture usage of that 'striving' by which we enter into life. The word is full of earnestness,—'Αγωνίζεσθε,—earnestness even to 'agony!'

[1] Mat., xi. 12. [2] Mark, ii. 2, 3. [3] Eph., vi. 11–18.
[4] Isa., lvii. 2. [5] Luke, xiii. 24.
[6] 1 Cor., ix. 24–27; 1 Tim., vi. 12.

Let us now see how this earnestness found expression. So shall we have another mark of true hearing.

III. When the gospel is heard aright, it *leads to prayer*. This was the first thing Bartimeus did, when he was told that Jesus was passing by,—he prayed. And this is always the first thing for a lost sinner who hears of Christ,—let him pray. A soul truly in earnest after salvation *will* cry for help. If a man feels his just exposure to wrath, he will be full of anguish, and his anguish will constrain him to cry out. For what is prayer but human need craving the divine fulness, the wretchedness of earth begging the consolations of heaven, man's guilt beseeching the mercy of God? By prayer the helplessness of the creature clings to the strength of the Creator. Prayer is a voice from nature's wound calling to the heavenly Healer.

Self-preservation is the first law of nature, and when our strength fails, prayer is nature's messenger for helpers. It may be the shriek of fright, the scream of torture, the imploring eye, the quivering lip, the clasped hands, the pleading tongue, or any of the thousand forms by which heart speaks to heart;—these are nature's prayers.

And when did nature fail to pray in her need? Hunger *will* beg and pain cry out. Though the fever have caused madness, the sufferer will still cry for water. None need teach the babe to clamor for its nurture. Birds can plead for their young, and the dog entreat you, with all the power of speech, to follow him to the forest where his master lies robbed and bleeding.

And has the soul no voice in its sickness unto death? Is the instinct of the brute a sure guide, and do the reason and conscience of men slumber or lie? Or are they quick-sighted and honest about bodily wants and earthly things, only to show themselves utterly besotted, when glory, honor and immortality are at stake? When your souls are in jeopardy, must you be plied with such urgency, before you will cry for help? Alas, I see you lying in the arms of Satan, bound hand and foot with his hellish fetters, and borne swiftly away into his region of outer darkness.[1] His cruel eye glares on you, in anticipation of the tortures he will soon begin on your helpless soul. Further and further from hope and heaven he bears you, the frown of God is on you, and the shadows of night are deepening around you. Thicker grows the gloom, when flash! flash! shoot up the flames of hell, as it is moved from beneath to meet you at your coming. Ah, why are you not terrified? Why do we hear no cry of alarm, no call for help? Does your *soul* know no law of self-preservation? Has it no instinct of terror? Does Reason see nothing fearful in the blackness of darkness, the pangs of undying remorse, the torments of unquenchable fire?[2] Can it be that you believe these things? You say you do, but can it be, when they do not move you to prayer? When God calls you from the secret place of thunder,[3] shall His voice be unregarded? When He declares that these things truly describe your woful state, will you

[1] 1 John, v. 19; "lieth in wickedness;" rather, (it is generally agreed,) "in the Wicked One." 2 Tim., ii. 26.; Eph., ii. 2.
[2] Jude, 13; Mark, ix. 43, 44, 45, 46, 47, 48.
[3] Psalm lxxxi. 7.

give Him the lie by your indifference, and still sleep on as you fast post to hell?

Sinners, be entreated to pray. You must pray or perish. No sinner ever went to heaven without prayer. God's curse is on the prayerless. The tongue that will not call on Him for mercy, shall consume in the fires of His wrath. Sleep now or not, you will not sleep long. If the voice of grace, sometimes warning, sometimes inviting, cannot wake you and bring you to your knees, God will try the voice of unmixed vengeance. He will see whether the shout of the archangel and the trump of God will fail. Ah! then you will wake, to sleep no more. Then you will come to your knees, for the weight of the Omnipotent hand will bring you down. The stoutest devil will bend and you will crouch beside him, for God has sworn by Himself that to Him every knee shall bow.[1] Then you will pray, but you had as well not, only you cannot help it.[2] You will pray like Dives,[3]—pray even to a man, you who now will not pray to God; pray for a drop of water, you

[1] Is., xlv. 23. [2] Prov., i. 24–28. [3] Luke, xvi. 23–26.

who now will not pray for heaven; pray for that poor drop at the hand of a despised beggar, you who now will not accept infinite blessings from the Hand that made the world, and was nailed to the Cross for our salvation! Thus shall you pray. But how will the answer pierce you with remorse and freeze you in despair. "Son, remember!" Compelled remembrance is the deathless sting of remorse. "A great gulf fixed!" There is the necessity and seal of unending despair. Pray then, pray! while you hear that "Jesus of Nazareth passeth by."

IV. And do it at once. *Promptness* is another mark of a good hearer of the gospel. It is found in Bartimeus. "And *when* he heard," that is, as soon as he heard, "he began to cry out."

But what need of such haste? "Jesus is going slowly," he might say, "and some little while must pass before He is gone. Be sure I will be in time."

Do you never reason so? "There is time enough yet. My life goes slowly; my health is firm; I shall certainly be in time."

Your life! your health!

> "Great God! on what a slender thread
> Hang everlasting things!"

"Or if he *does* get a little out of sight," Bartimeus might say, "while I am attending to some little matters, I will run after Him and call Him. I will never think of letting Him get out of *hearing*. I will be in time."

And is not this your way? Are you not letting mercies and opportunities slip by, and running the frightful risk that they may all pass away, and leave you on a death-bed, to call, in helpless agitation and dismay, for Sabbaths and sermons and Jesus Christ, rejected often, and now gone beyond your call—gone for ever?

"But I only want a *little* time, and that for most important business," Bartimeus might plead.

Why man, what business *can* you have now, but getting your blind eyes opened?

"O that *is* the chief thing to be sure, and I mean to attend to that. It would never do to neglect that greatest of matters. Ah, would that they were open now! But really, I must go about in this crowd for a few minutes, and collect what alms I can. I must live!"

Before any of you undertakes to rebuke this supposed reply too harshly, see if he had not more cause than you think, for such a course; nay, if he had not all the reasons that men now urge for neglecting their salvation.

Begging was his regular business, the only way he had of supporting himself, and possibly, a helpless family. Is not that excuse thought a good one in this day? Did you never use it? Is it not often heard in this form?—"I am in a business in which I *can't* be a Christian. I am connected with the railroad, or the Post-Office, and am required to labor on the Sabbath. I am very sorry it is so, and I mean some day to get out of it and attend to religion."

Would to God our groaning land were delivered from the curse of Sunday mails and Sunday railway trains, and all the oppressions and abominations they drag after them! But while they last, the duty of men, who fear God and mean to save their souls, is clear; and that is, to protest against them, pray against them, and above all, stand aloof from them, if they would not have the blood of God's "murdered Sabbaths" staining their skirts and crying from the ground for vengeance. Whatever your business, if it stands in the way of your serving God, it is wrong, and you must give it up, or keep it at the cost of losing Christ.[1] It may try you sorely, but you had better pluck out a right eye, or cut off a right hand, than be cast into hell.[2]

I miss the honest face of a German, who used to be in his seat every Sabbath morning and night, listening anxiously to the Word of God. For many years he had faithfully served one of our railroad companies through seven days of the week. But at length his conscience was awakened, and he could no longer serve them on the Sabbath. Six days he would labor hard, but God's day he must *have* for God. So he gave up his place. It was in the winter of 1854–5 too, when thousands of

[1] Mat., vi. 24; xvi. 24. [2] Mat., v. 29, 30.

workmen were thrown out of employment, and when men already out had almost no hope of getting in. But in the face of all this he gave up his place. Then month after month passed by, and brought no relief; not one dollar could he earn. The savings of years of toil were fast consuming, and soon his family would be suffering, and still he *could* not get employment. Then his old place was offered him, and it was a sore temptation. But God's Law stood up in his way, and bade him beware. So he was strengthened, and still trusted in God and obeyed His Word. For long months more were his faith and patience tried, until at last, with a reluctant but determined heart, he left the city, and sought in the far West a new home, where by the sweat of his brow he might earn his bread, and still have "freedom to worship God."

If all true men would do likewise, God would soon right their wrongs. He would teach our government and these huge corporations that, though they have joined hand in hand to defy the God of heaven, they shall not go unpunished. He is yet a God that judgeth in the earth. As they tempt men to transgression, He will brand them with the curse of Jeroboam, the son of Nebat, who made Israel to sin.[1] He will set His face against them in dreadful Providences. He has dealt with our nation as He did with Israel of old, in great goodness. We may yet have to learn, as they have, in exile and tears, His severity also.[2] And these powerful companies will find that, if their requirements and God's come in conflict, their best servants will leave them, and then their places of high trust must be filled by those who fear not God, and therefore regard not man,[3] and then swift damage and ruin must come upon them, until they repent and learn righteousness.

Meantime, let all who suffer for conscience' sake take this good word of Christ for their consolation; Verily I say unto you, there is no man that hath left house, or parents, or brethren, or wife, or children for the Kingdom of God's sake, who shall not receive mani-

[1] 1 Kings, xii. 26–30; xiii. 34. [2] Rom., xi. 22.
[3] Luke, xviii. 4.

fold more in this present time, and in the world to come, life everlasting![1]

But if Bartimeus choose to attend to his alms instead of his eyes, see if he has not a still stronger reason. Begging is not only his business, but this happens to be a very "busy season," as we say in the city, or "harvest-time," as they say in the country. A multitude was passing! When had he such a chance before? He waits day after day, glad of an occasional traveller; but to-day the people pour along in crowds, and can he afford to leave his business now? Sight is no doubt a very good thing; but suppose all these people should give him even a penny a-piece,—think of that! He might go home almost rich,—might almost retire from business! And after all has not Providence given him this opportunity, and would it be exactly *right* to throw it away?

So have I heard professors of religion and non-professors reason. So do they put earth's business above all the calls of God. With such words do some members of the Church

[1] Luke, xviii. 29, 30.

throw all the active work of the Church on some one else; yes, on others as busy as you, or at least, as busy as you have any right to be. They redeem time, or take time at a sacrifice, which you could take, and should, and would, if your hearts were right before God. Some of you make business and busy seasons, (which seem to last most of the year,) an excuse for not seeking God, and some, for not serving Him, despite all your professions and vows. Some of you are too much pressed ever to get to prayer-meetings, or the services before the holy Communion, to do any of the work of the Church, by which her influence is enlarged, her wheels are made to move on, and by which your graces might be enriched and manifested.

In the dark ages men sometimes sold themselves by deliberate compact to the devil. For so much wealth or honor he should have their souls. Men rarely do that now, I suppose, in any formal way. But this busy age, busy country, and busy city, are binding them in chains, and sealing them for hell, as surely as any infernal sorceries. When men say they have no time for religion, while they acknowledge its divine claims, they really say, "Business, be thou my God! I devote myself to thee."

Men of the world! You must take time for religion, or eternity for remorse. If you take the world for your service, you must take hell for your reward.[1]

Men of the Church! Your whole time is God's, and you must use it for His glory, so as to satisfy, not only your ungodly business-partner, and your torpid conscience, but the severities of the Judgment Bar. If you do not always make the world's calls yield to Christ's, then you deny your Saviour and belie your profession.[2]

But let me no longer misrepresent Bartimeus, even in supposition. He delays not, but makes haste.

Christ is passing, and he *may* be too late, and therefore he is in haste.

He is blind and feels the misery of blindness, and therefore he is in haste.

If he begs first, Christ may be insulted by

1 Luke, xvi. 25. 2 Mat., x. 37–39.

this putting of filthy lucre before His healing power, and so may refuse the blessing when it *is* sought,[1] and therefore he is in haste.

And sinner, be you in haste. There is a limit to God's long-suffering. He will not see His calls made light of for ever. He will not stand waiting all the day long. His Providence and grace will move on. His voice will be silent. He will noiselessly withdraw, and you shall call after Him and grope after Him for ever, but never find Him again![2]

V. and VI. Two other marks of a good hearer of the gospel are found in Bartimeus. He heard with *Faith and Humility*. He trusted in Jesus and was lowly in heart. He felt his need and looked to Christ for aid. Humility laid him in the dust, while Faith reached up and took hold on the strength of the Redeemer.

His faith even outran the word of the multitude. They spoke of "Jesus of Nazareth," —Nazareth of Galilee—a despised town of a despised province; but *he* could call Him "Son of David," and "Lord." In these words

[1] Heb., xii. 16. 17. [2] Prov., i. 24–31.

he hailed Him as the Messiah, the promised Messiah of God, of whom Isaiah had foretold that He should open the eyes of the blind.[1] Though Nathanael might ask, Can any good thing come out of Nazareth?[2] and the Pharisees assert that, Out of Galilee there ariseth no prophet,[3] this poor blind man had an eye of faith which saw in Him, the great descendant of David who should redeem Israel,—David's Son and David's Lord.[4] He believed too that He was now passing by, and that He had power enough and love enough to open his eyes. This was his simple faith, and by this he took hold on Christ for deliverance.

And how deep was his humility! He hid nothing, pretended nothing. He came as he was. Blind, he came as blind. Poor, he came as poor. A beggar, he came as a beggar. He set up no claim as of right. He told of no good deed. But needy and wretched and helpless and unworthy, he cast himself on the tender heart of Christ; "Jesus, Son of David, have mercy on me! O Lord, Son of David, have mercy on me!"

[1] Is., xxxv. 5; xlii. 7. [2] John, i. 46.
[3] John, vii. 52 [4] Mat., xxii. 45.

But is this the whole lesson? When we have found both faith and humility in this prayer, are we to view them apart only? May either be absent, and are they here in friendly meeting but by chance?

No: the prayer has a deeper and more precious teaching. Faith and humility are so blended in it, that none can say how much is one, and how much the other. If faith is more manifest in the titles he gives Christ, yet humility is not wanting; and if humility shines brightest in his asking for "mercy," faith is seen in his simple reliance on that mercy.

And so it is always. Faith and humility meet in the sinner's experience, not as occasional companions only; they ever walk lovingly together as sisters. They cannot separate. Like the Siamese twins they live in each other's presence alone; should they part, they would die. A sinner cannot believe in Jesus and not be humble; he cannot be truly humble without believing in Jesus.

This is most needful for a sinner to know; for when seeking Christ, he fears it would be presumptuous to believe and rest on Christ at once. So he still stays away and tries to prepare himself for Christ. He thinks that this is true humility; but it is only pride in disguise, and so deceiving him.

"Alas, I am lost," begins the sinner, "what shall I do to be saved?"[1]

"Come to me," says Christ, "I came to seek and save that which was lost."[2]

"But how can I come? I am a sinner."

"Come *because* you are a sinner. I came not to call the righteous, but sinners to repentance."[3]

"But I am *such* a sinner," says this false humility, (for you see it dares dispute with Christ,) "there never was a heart as bad as mine."

"The greater your sin, the greater your need of me," says Christ, "and do not fear, for I came into the world to save sinners, even the chief. This is a faithful saying, and worthy of all acceptation."[4]

"But my heart is so *hard*."

[1] Acts, xvi. 30. [2] Luke, xix. 10.
[3] Luke, v. 32. [4] 1 Tim., i. 15.

"Then give it to me, and I will soften it, I will take away the stony heart out of your flesh, and I will give you an heart of flesh."[1]

"But I do not even feel my sins as I ought," continues this disputatious, arrogant humility.

"And you never will," answers Christ, "until you have a new heart; come to me, and I will give you one."[2]

"But I cannot see *any thing* good in my heart; I am *too* unworthy; I have no faith, no love."

"Then come without them," says Christ, "and I will give them to you."[3]

But the heart is not ready to give up yet, and take Christ just at His word. It cannot understand that it is to go to Christ with absolutely nothing to recommend it, and so it toils on with huge pains and anxiety, to do something, or be something, or feel something, which shall make it more fit to come to Christ. So after a while Christ comes again and says very kindly, "Poor heart, you can never

[1] Ezek., xxxvi. 26. [2] *Ibid.* [3] Gal., v. 22, with Acts, ii. 33.

make yourself better. Only I can do that. If you come at all, it must be just as you are."

"Alas! alas! I wish I could, but I seem to get worse and worse."

"But do you believe, or not, that I am able to save you?" says Christ.

"Oh, yes! *You* are able, but *I* am so unworthy."

And so this blind self-righteousness reasons round and round in a circle, and still comes back to the same fatal point, and though very sad, takes a secret comfort in being so very humble!

Now Christ comes again, and speaks searching words, but very patiently; "Blind and stubborn heart, I will show you a little of yourself. You say you believe I am able to save all sinners; able to save you. But you do not, or you would trust me to be your Saviour. You could trust me to save a softer heart, or a better heart, or a heart that felt more; but not your hard, wicked heart. Does not this limit my power, my grace, my blood? Am I a Saviour for little sins, and not for great?[1] Does your unworthiness overtop my Righteousness?[2] Does my blood fail for your heart?[3] My Righteousness and blood are infinite,[4] and do you stretch up to measure them and find them wanting? I say I *can* save you, and what arrogance it is that denies it! What boundless presumption! If you were better you would come, you say. Yes; you are too proud to come as other sinners. You must needs be an exception. You cannot be altogether indebted to grace. A *little* worthiness must be found, for the glory and comfort of your self-righteousness. Abase yourself in the dust, and come just as you are."

If these cutting words of Christ slay the sinner's pride, true humility fills his heart. *It* dares not dispute with Christ, or think of making any change in His plan of grace, amazing as its freeness seems. It just takes Him at His word, and says,

"Just as I am, without one plea,
But that Thy blood was shed for me,
And that Thou bidst me come to Thee,
O Lamb of God, I come!

[1] Isa., i. 18. [2] Rom., x. 4. [3] 1 John, i. 7.
[4] Jer., xxiii. 6; Heb., vii. 25.

"Just as I am, and waiting not,
To rid my soul of one dark blot,
To Thee whose blood can cleanse each spot,
O Lamb of God, I come!

"Just as I am,—poor, wretched, blind—
Sight, riches, healing of the mind,
Yea, all I need, in Thee to find,
O Lamb of God, I come!"

Thus do these holy sisters, Faith and Humility, go together to Christ. When Humility, looking down upon her sins, would faint in the way, Faith feels the pressure of her drooping form, and lifting her own clear eye to the glories of Christ, bids her look to Him and be comforted. And even Faith grows bolder, when Humility in her turn whispers, "Do not fear; though our sins are many,[1] *He* can cleanse them. If He says Come, we cannot but take Him at His word." And Humility grows lowlier, when Faith drawing near, and fixing her eye on Calvary, says, "Oh sister, against what a Saviour we have sinned!"

[1] Psalm ciii. 3, 11; Luke, vii. 47.

IV.

"And many charged him that he should hold his peace; but he cried the more a great deal, Thou Son of David, have mercy upon me!"

THERE is never a knock at heaven's gate, but it sounds through hell, and devils come out to silence it.[1] Whenever a soul is striving for heaven, or heaven striving for a soul, which is but another side of the same truth, there two worlds are at strife.[2] The Mohammedans have a saying that, whenever two persons meet, there is always a third. The proverb refers to the presence of God. But it is just as true that when God and a human soul meet on business for eternity, Satan will be there. He will be there as an opposer and destroyer.[3] All souls are his at first,[4] for by *nature* we are

[1] 1 Pet., v. 8. [2] Mat., xiii. 37, 39; Eph., vi. 11, 12; 1 John, iv. 4. [3] 2 Cor., ii. 11; Luke, viii. 12.
[4] Eph., ii. 2; John, viii. 44.

children of wrath;[1] and he never lets his own go without a struggle.[2] He hath the cheek-teeth of a great lion, and it is not easy to rend the prey from his mouth.[3]

Both Christ and Satan came on earth as destroyers; Satan to destroy the works of God, but Christ to destroy *his* destructions and the destroyer himself.[4] And so we must look for war on the earth, and must ourselves take part in the battle, if we mean to go to heaven.[5] The kingdom of heaven suffereth violence, and the violent taketh it by force.[6]

The children of Israel sang bravely on the shore of the Red Sea, and behaved themselves stoutly. They seemed just ready to go up and possess the promised land. But the howling wilderness soon shut up their song, and when they began to hear of giants and war chariots of iron, and cities walled up to heaven, their craven hearts died within them, and for base safety, beside full flesh-pots, they were ready to slink back into slavery.[7]

[1] Eph., ii. 3. [2] Mark, ix. 20, 25, 26.
[3] Mark, ix. 29. [4] Rev., xii. 12; Heb., ii. 14; 1 John, iii. 8.
[5] Eph., vi. 11–18. [6] Mat., xi. 12.
[7] Ex., xv. 1–21.; xvi. 1–3; Deut., i. 27, 28.

The giants are not all dead yet, and if a pilgrim do but show himself, going toward the City of God, out they come to give him battle. So, those who mean to serve Christ, may as well make up their minds at once to meet opposition.[1]

Bartimeus had sad proof of this. As soon as he began to cry out for mercy, rebukes rained down upon him from all sides. Satan raised a clamor, and tried to beat him down. Am I not right in ascribing this opposition to the old murderer, though men were his agents? What was the offence? A sightless beggar beseeches the compassion of the Heavenly Physician. He has never been near Him before. This is the only opportunity of his life. A word or touch can heal him, and in a sudden agony of earnestness, he begs the blessed stranger to pity him,—said I not rightly, that none but a devil would have bidden him hold his peace?

But Satan hides while he works. He is sometimes like a lion roaring on his prey,[2] but oftener a serpent gliding in the grass,

[1] 2 Tim., iii. 12. [2] 1 Pet., v. 8.

biting, gone.[1] He can even put on the form of an angel of light,[2] and here he wears the guise of the followers of Christ.

There is a manifold, hellish craft in this. He conceals himself, puts the shame of his deeds on the cause of God, destroys his victims more easily and surely because his hand is not seen, corrupts all who do his work, and thus brings them under his own condemnation, and fills many who see what is done, with such prejudice against the cause and followers of Christ, that they too are ruined.

The ungodly world bids anxious souls to hold their peace. It cannot bear the sinner's distress. If *his* conscience is disturbed its own is not quite easy. If he cries out through fear of the wrath to come,[3] a shudder passes through *its* heart. If he speaks of heaven, it is not ready, it feels, for that, and its own joys look pale in that pure light. If the weight of eternal concernments smite him amidst its gay throngs, it has the unpleasant effect of the sudden death of an actor in the Theatre. The play goes on, to be sure, but the applause is

[1] 2 Cor., xi. 3. [2] 2 Cor., xi. 14. [3] Mat., iii. 7.

not hearty, and a chill shadow damps the mirth. The tragedy is gloomy and the comedy hollow.

Therefore the world sets itself to make an end of these convictions. For this it has innumerable devices. It will flatter, or curse. For some it has persecutions, for others promotions. Now it laughs with irresistible merriment; now dazzles with deceitful splendors, and now cuts one's acquaintance with a sneer. It bewilders the reason with sophistry, and bewitches the senses with voluptuousness. And two other foes it brings into the field for the silencing of crying souls,—Infidelity, with its thousand 'phases,' (changing every day,) its flippancy, its sarcasms, its dogmatism, (which never change;) and Atheism, with its sullen front and frozen heart.

But I pause not on any of these. I wish now to address the *professed people of God.* I pray you heed an honest warning.

I say then plainly: *You* are in great danger, every day, of rebuking anxious souls, and charging them to hold their peace. I do not say you do it wittingly. It is a sin so awful, so unnatural, so cruel, that every lover of the Saviour must utterly abhor it. Yet even Christ's true friends may commit it carelessly and unconsciously. Bear then some cautions.

I. By *injudicious criticism of sermons* you may stifle convictions and drive sinners away from Christ.

We do not refuse to be tried by honest and enlightened judgments; and when we hear their verdict, it should give us little concern, except to learn how we may become wiser and more faithful stewards of the mysteries of God.[1] But we charge our hearers not to forget that, however humble our abilities, if we are in our place at all, we are Ambassadors for Christ,[2] standing in His room, making known His terms of pardon; and that, so far as we preach the Word,[3] He will take its vindication into His own hands, and avenge it of every slight and all contempt.[4]

Nay more; when we preach Christ crucified, our message is the power of God, by

[1] 1 Cor., iv. 1. [2] 2 Cor., v. 20.
[3] 2 Tim., iv. 2. [4] Luke, x. 16; ix. 26.

which alone sinners can be saved; but your criticisms may turn it into very foolishness, and a stumbling-block, and the savor of death to some beloved one for whose salvation you have been striving.[1]

I cannot better illustrate this caution than by a true narrative from "The Central Presbyterian." "A pious lady once left a church in this city, [Richmond,] in company with her husband, who was not a professor of religion. She was a woman of unusual vivacity, with a keen perception of the ludicrous, and often playfully sarcastic. As they walked along toward home, she began to make some amusing and spicy comments on the sermon, which a stranger, a man of very ordinary talents and awkward manner, had preached, that morning, in the absence of the pastor. After running on in this vein of sportive criticism for some time, surprised at the profound silence of her husband, she turned and looked up in his face. He was in tears. That sermon had sent an arrow of conviction to his heart! What must have been the anguish of the

[1] Cor., i. 23, 24, 2 Cor., ii. 16.

conscience-stricken wife, thus arrested in the act of ridiculing a discourse which had been the means of awakening the anxiety of her unconverted husband!"

Watch then, your words and spirit. Take care what you say, and before whom you say it. Are you about to speak in love, in humility, in the temper of Christ? Will any one be the better for what you say? Will your criticisms deepen your child's or your friend's reverence for Christ's Ambassadors, and God's chosen instrument for saving souls? When you have said what you wish, will you become thereby fellow-helpers to the truth?[1] If not, oh, leave it all unsaid, lest in criticising the flaws of the earthen vessel, you be found to have despised the heavenly treasure;[2] lest you turn aside the sword of the Spirit,[3] and with great sin to yourself, bring destruction on some most precious soul.

II. Beware also of *unseasonable levity after solemn appeals.*

I do not warn you against cheerfulness. It is pleasant to see the faces of God's people

[1] 3 John 8. [2] 2 Cor., iv. 7. [3] Eph., vi. 17.

beaming with the secret refreshments of the Spirit, or reflecting the glories which shine from between the cherubim.[1] But this sacred rejoicing is no more like levity, than the clear diffused light of morning is like the flash of shaken tinsel. Cheerfulness is the genial warmth of the Sun of Righteousness;[2] levity the crackling of thorns under a pot.[3] One is the voice of rejoicing which becometh the tabernacles of the righteous,[4] the other the laughter of fools, fit only for the tents of wickedness.[5] Cheerfulness can mingle with solemnity, just as the clear heavens may be solemn with night, yet cheerful with stars.

A Christian can sit in God's House, and relish all the truths of His Word. He may indeed often hear what is immediately distressing. Unlike the little book which the angel gave John, it may be bitter and painful in the mouth, that is, in the hearing; yet being mixed with faith, it shall through grace be sweet and wholesome in the digestion.[6] In the very thunders of Sinai he will hear the

[1] Ps. lxxx. 1. [2] Mal., iv. 2. [3] Eccl., vii. 6.
[4] Ps. cxviii. 15. [5] Ps. lxxxiv. 10. [6] Rev., x. 9

voice of his covenant God,[1] and prostrate himself in holy abasement. If God be set forth as a consuming fire,[2] taking vengeance, he will confess that this is but his own desert;[3] and while adoring the sovereign grace which has saved him from wrath, he will be grieved for transgressors,[4] and weep for them, and pray for them; and when the congregation breaks up, and he meets them face to face, there will be something in his eye and voice and pressure of the hand, which will touch sinners to the heart, with a sense of their own danger, and the affectionate anxiety of God's people.

How different the conduct of many professors! They may be dull enough while the word is preached, but when the benediction is pronounced, how relieved and lively they seem! With what alacrity they address themselves to the business of leaving the Church! With what sprightliness are the aisles suddenly animated! And so with jests and vanity and levity they go to their homes, sit at their tables, and hold mirthful converse with their unconverted children and friends.

[1] Ex., xx. 2. [2] Heb., xii. 29. [3] Ps. li. 4. [4] Ps. cxix. 158

Ah! in some breast at that table the struggle for eternity may have begun; the Spirit of God and the powers of darkness may be engaged in their final conflict, and this foolish jesting may decide it for despair and hell! What a fearful truth! One may laugh away the Holy Ghost and all conviction of sin, laugh the awakened conscience to sleep and precious souls to perdition!

III. This brings to mind another way by which you may bid sinners hold their peace,—by *blindness to any beginning concern.*

If you do not watch for the Spirit, He may pass by unseen. If He is not cherished, He may pass away. A great part of this cherishing work belongs to you, as disciples of Christ and friends of the Spirit. By mere neglect you may ruin the work in which you were called to be workers together with God.[1] You fail to come up to the help of the Lord,[2] and so your friend may be lost.

Would you see *how* you should watch? Come with me to the chamber where a babe lies dying. A breathless messenger has gone

[1] 2 Cor., vi. 1. [2] Judges, v. 23.

for the physician, but still he comes not. How the worn mother gazes on her little sufferer in an agony of fondness and fear; how she sinks in anguish before the mercy-seat, and pleads like the Syrophenician woman at the feet of Jesus;[1] how she rises wildly, and watches at the window for the physician; how at every sound of wheels she flushes with eagerness, and then grows sick at heart as they turn the corner, and the sound dies away; how she springs to the door as his well-known step is heard on the stair; and then, as he searches every symptom, how she waits on his every look, living on a gleam of hope, ready to die if his face is darkened by a cloud!

O disciple of Jesus, thy child, thy brother, some beloved of thine, is sick unto eternal death; and where is this watching for the Great Physician? this weeping, longing, praying? Ah, when He has of His own heart's love come near, and alarmed the dying soul from its fatal torpor, and prescribed His sovereign remedies, you will not even be nursing fathers and mothers,[2] to carry on the Lord's

1 Mat., xv. 22–28. 2 Is., xlix. 23.

gracious work, and save these dear souls from death!

IV. Nor is this the worst. Professing parents often *lay plans for their children directly opposed to the Spirit's work.*

Let one example illustrate my meaning. In your morning devotions you ask God to convert your children—even on the next Sabbath to send His word with power to their hearts. Surely you should pray so, and I will suppose you do. But, before the day is over, yielding to the tide of corrupt worldliness around you, or the pleadings of your unconverted children, you arrange for a dancing-party the next week, and issue your invitations. "Only a children's dancing-party, and only with the piano, you know," you say patronizingly and cheerfully to conscience, though somehow conscience looks a little blank at these nice distinctions, and does not return your smile. But let that pass. Suppose, however, God answers your prayer on the Sabbath, and one of these children weeps under the sermon, and comes home downcast and distressed; what will your condition be? To say the least, will you feel no embarrassment? No temptation to seem not to have observed it, until your scheme is carried out? No regret even, that these feelings should have come just then? How awkward that when you had meant your daughter to be so bright and beautiful in the dance on Monday, that she should be convicted of sin, and fleeing from God's wrath, and weeping so, on Sunday! On the other hand, will you have no fear lest the excitements of the giddy scene shall quench the Spirit,[1] and harden the heart for ever?[2] And, besides all this, would not these convictions take you by surprise, and send a guilty pang to your heart? *Could* you be, as you ought always to be, expecting in strong faith the answer of your prayers, and ready to bless God with a clear heart, and go in secret with this dear anxious soul, and mingle your tears, and together beseech Christ for mercy?

But how can I exhaust the ways by which professed Christians may bid troubled sinners hold their peace? By all your worldly-

[1] 1 Thess., v. 19. [2] Heb., iii. 13.

mindedness and worldly-conformity; by every proof you give that you think more of this life than of that to come; that you will spend more, sacrifice more, go through more to gain earthly ends than for Christ and His cause; by all these you become stumbling-blocks in the way of sinners coming to Christ.

These too, are the things you cannot hide. Some very pious looks and tones for special seasons; some very common-place Christian observations now and then; some very general sighing over the fact that 'We all come short,' &c., &c., none of these will do. Your little children and your servants see the inconsistency.

O this worldliness in professors! This want of whole-conformity to Christ![1] This is the most grievous stain on Christianity, the hardest argument of infidelity, the greatest hindrance of revivals, and their surest extinguisher. Because of this hath the Lord covered the daughter of Zion with a cloud in His anger. For this her ways mourn, her gates are desolate, her priests sigh, her virgins are

[1] Rom., xii. 1, 2.

afflicted, and she is in bitterness; while her enemies blaspheme, and all that pass by clap their hands at her; they hiss and wag their head at the daughter of Jerusalem![1]

Now let me sound an honest alarm to all of every name and condition, who in any way charge convicted sinners to hold their peace. You are opposing the work of God, and must beware of His heavy arm. If you are His people and your opposition is unwitting, He will teach you needful lessons by the Voice of the Rod.[2] They may be very hard,[3] but you will have to learn them.[4] He will not suffer such sin upon you.[5] But if you are not His people, you shall feel his vengeance. You are falling on the eternal corner-stone and shall be broken; and unless you speedily cease to oppose those who would build upon it, and begin yourself to build there, that stone shall one day fall upon you and grind you to powder![6]

There is no sadder doom than theirs who

[1] Lamentations.
[2] Mic., vi. 9; Ps. cxix. 67, 71.
[3] Heb., xii. 11.
[4] Prov., iii. 12; Rev., iii. 19.
[5] Heb., xii. 10.
[6] Mat., xxi. 44.

lead men into sin, or keep souls from Christ. It is enough to go to hell at all. But if I must go, let me go alone. Let me not carry my tormentors with me. Its fires will be hot enough, and its woes heavy enough, without souls whom I have ruined, to heap them upon me in revenge for ever pitiless, and exasperated for ever by their own eternal agony. If I am bent on death, let me like Ahithophel, put my household in order and die alone,[1] and not like Samson gather the pillars of the temple in my grasp, and drag others down with me, myself falling undermost and buried in the deepest ruin.[2]

Now let me say two things to awakened sinners.

Are you thus opposed? If you fail, this will not excuse you. One man's sin may be another's temptation and his ruin, but it can never be his apology. Satan tempted Eve, and she tempted Adam, but all three of them were cursed.[3] Even the heathen could say, The gods help those who help themselves; and we may be sure that Christ will help every soul

[1] 2 Sam., xvii. 23. [2] Judges, xvi. 30. [3] Gen., iii. 12–19

in earnest after Him. God has never said to the seed of Jacob, Seek ye me in vain.[1] Seek, says Christ, and ye *shall* find.[2] When God calls a soul out of Egypt, old tyrants and new enemies, a deep sea and a howling wilderness may all be in the way, but if that soul be of good courage it shall not fail to eat of the golden fruits of Canaan.[3] Neither the chosen people nor a chosen soul ever lost a battle except by cowardice or sin. For His mercy endureth for ever;—twenty-six times over is that said in the Psalm that recounts Israel's redemption and triumphs.[4] At every point, at every danger and every battle is the story interrupted to say, For His mercy endureth for ever! Has God said to you, Seek ye my face? And has your heart replied, Thy face, Lord, will I seek?[5] Then, though a host should encamp against you, your heart need not fear. Though father and mother forsake you, the God of your salvation will never leave you nor forsake you.[6] So, wait upon

[1] Is., xlv. 19.
[2] Mat., vii. 7, 8.
[3] Joshua, v. 11, 12.
[4] Ps. cxxxvi.
[5] Ps. xxvii. 8.
[6] Ps. xxvii. 3, 10; Heb., xiii. 5

the Lord; be of good courage, and He shall strengthen your heart! Wait, I say, on the Lord.[1]

Are you thus opposed? Do as Bartimeus did. "He cried the more," says Matthew; "the more a great deal," or "so much the more," say Mark and Luke. O that is brave! Opposition only rouses him to new energy. And so cry you. It is time to "cry out" when men would beat you back from Christ; time to summon all your strength when the enemy is summoning his. See! there is but one way; the path is narrow; the foe is closing in. Now soul, if thou wouldst not be lost, quit thyself like a man.[2] Take shield and sword, and lay about thee. It is now or never with thee. Cry unto Christ and press forward. And while using all thy might, still remember that nothing can cut through the foe and clear thy path to Christ, like this cry of faith, "Jesus, Son of David, have mercy upon me!"

[1] Ps. xxvii. 14. [2] 1 Cor., xvi. 13.

V.

"And Jesus stood still and called him."—(Matthew.)

"And Jesus stood still and commanded him to be called."—(Mark.)

"And Jesus stood and commanded him to be brought unto Him."—(Luke.)

WHEN Jesus thus "stood still," He was on His way for the last time to Jerusalem. His "hour" was drawing nigh,[1] and He was hastening to meet it. He knew it was to be an hour of anguish and desertion, the hour and power of darkness.[2] He saw the cup He was to drink, and He knew the bitterness of every drop.[3] He knew He was to wrestle with the terrors of death and the principalities of hell, and bear the insufferable torments of avenging wrath. Yet such love for sinners, such hatred of sin, such zeal for the vindication of the insulted glory of the Godhead filled and

[1] John, xvii. 1; Mark, xiv. 41. [2] Luke, xxii. 53.
[3] Mark, x. 32–34; Mat., xx. 22; xxvi. 39; John, xviii. 11.

fired Him, that He was pressing on, with almost impatient ardor. He was straitened, in an inexpressible way, till He had offered Himself a sacrifice to Divine justice for the sins of His people.[1]

Never was any being in the universe on such a journey before. Never can even He be again. The redemption of the world,[2] the defeat of Satan,[3] and the most illustrious display of the Attributes of God which ever can be made,[4] the infinite concernments of three worlds, heaven, earth and hell, and the glory of the sovereign, eternal Godhead, all rested on Him and the decease He was about to accomplish at Jerusalem.[5]

Can He be arrested in *this* journey? Where is the event mighty enough to stay His course? What destiny of man or empire is worthy even of a thought from Him now? Shall not the vision of infinite suffering, and the infinite glory that is to follow,[6] absorb His heart? Avaunt, even ye angels of God! Let not cherubim or seraphim intrude now!

[1] Luke, xii. 50. [2] John, i. 29. [3] Heb., ii. 14.
[4] Luke, ii. 14; John, xiii. 31; xvii. 1, 4, 6; Eph., iii. 10, 21.
[5] Luke, ix. 31. [6] 1 Pet., i. 11.

Be astonished, O ye heavens, and be silent, O earth, while your Maker and Lord, who is over all, God blessed for ever,[1] treads His path of unutterable shame and glory! He must walk that awful way alone!

But what voice breaks this holy silence? Who dares draw so near, with clamors so loud? A degraded mortal! A miserable, blind beggar! obtruding *his* petty sorrows on the Heart that is gathering to itself the woes of a world! Can he be regarded? Will the war-chariot, rushing into battle, turn aside for a worm? Will the swell of the sea, roaring on the shore, be checked lest a lamb be drowned? Shall we not join with the multitude and bid Bartimeus hold his peace?

Ah, if we do, neither we nor they know the heart of our Lord. If we mean thus to do Him honor, we will find we have only put ourselves to shame. For see, He turns to the cry; He looks upon the beggar. There is no lightning in His eye, no terror in His voice. His sorrowful face beams with benignity. He stands still. His journey *is* stayed. He calls

[1] Rom., ix. 5.

the poor man to Him, and gently directs those about Him to repeat His welcoming words and guide the uncertain steps to Him.

"He stood still." Let us also stand and admire. Here let us learn the grace of our Redeemer, and lay up in our hearts the blessed teaching.

Is not the scene beautiful? Is not the grandeur of such calmness Godlike; the gracefulness of such condescension worthy of a birth in heaven? Can it be less than celestial radiance that streams out in such benevolence?

Then may we learn how unreasonable and how unnatural is a favorite clamor of infidels against the gospel. They say they cannot believe that the Son of God came to this world and died for its redemption. This world is too small and mean in the great scale of the universe, to allow them to think that the creator of countless millions of glorious suns and systems, could have stooped to love and care and suffer and die for the poor creatures of a day, who live on this insignificant planet.

This objection taken from the discoveries of

Astronomy, Dr. Chalmers has swept away, in his own magnificent manner, in his Astronomical Discourses, and I shall not attempt "the height of his great argument." Neither does it suit my present design to enter on a long discussion. But if the naturalness and beauty of this scene near Jericho be granted, does it not throw light on that tremendous tragedy which the gospel declares to have been enacted on Calvary? Granting,—as who will not?—that no violence is done in *this* scene to any of our ideas of the becoming and beautiful, but rather that we have here a most attractive blending of grace, condescension and heavenly charity, may not the Cross itself be granted, and its Divine Sufferer?

To a narrow vision a structure may seem unsightly from its vastness, while in miniature the same eye might find the proportions exquisite. And have we not, in this standing still of Jesus, amidst the urgencies of such a journey, at the call of a beggar, a miniature of the very things by which some are confounded or repelled, in the immense transactions of the Atonement? It was worthy of the illustrious Stranger—nay, it was beautiful, it was sublime—to stay for the relief of the unhappy beggar, though His own mind was burdened with the weight of the infinite sacrifice He was about to offer. Then who shall so vilify the redemption of men by the Cross, as to pronounce it unworthy of the Sovereign of a universe to which our earth is but an atom? Shall an Astronomer be so lost in God's glory declared by the heavens,[1] in their measureless and bright immensity, as to scorn the thought of His upholding and blessing each sun and star? Then if these philosophers gaze on the luminous, illimitable fields of creation, until their dazzled minds turn back with contempt to the world on which they dwell, and find no worth nor grandeur in the Cross which redeems it, though it saves numbers without number from perdition, and glorifies them in the light of God, and displays His Attributes before an admiring universe, let us hold up the confessed truthfulness and beauty of this simple incident, till, "like a mirror of diamond, it pierce

[1] Psalm xix. 1.

their misty eye-balls"[1] and lead them on to the acknowledgment of the truth.

"Jesus stood still," and when did He ever refuse to stay at the call of the distressed sinner? Nay, if He stayed then, when *can* He refuse? Is He not the same, yesterday, today and for ever?[2] Has the love, which death and the grave could not quench, perished in His exaltation?[3] Did He not bring it with Him from the Throne? Or rather, did it not bring Him from the Throne?[4] And is it not an everlasting love? O needy sinner, He cannot refuse your cry. "Jesus, Son of David, have mercy on me," finds its way through the adoring ranks of saints and angels, and constrains His gracious heart. He cannot resist it. He has bound Himself in covenant to regard it.[5] Every thing else shall give way, if need be, but it shall prevail. Heaven and earth shall pass away, but not His word of promise to a sinner.[6]

The fires of eternal vengeance stood still

[1] Milton. Ref. in Eng. Book I.
[2] Heb., xiii. 8.
[3] John, xiii. 1; xiv. 1–3.
[4] Phil., ii. 6–8.
[5] John, xiv. 13, 14.
[6] Mat., xxiv. 35.

over Sodom till Lot was gone out.[1] The waves stood still, and the depths were congealed in the heart of the sea till the children of Israel passed over.[2] The down-rushing waters of swollen Jordan stood still, as the feet of the priests touched their brim, and rose up as a wall till the chosen tribes had gained their inheritance.[3] At the cry of Joshua, the sun stood still in the midst of the heavens, and the moon in the valley of Ajalon, until the Lord's hosts had avenged themselves upon their enemies.[4] And at the prayers and tears of Hezekiah, Time, whose onward urgency is the most inexorable of all things, not only stood still, but retreated. Ten degrees backward did the shadow go on the sun-dial of Ahaz, and fifteen years were added to the life of the dying king.[5]

But ah, me! death is swifter than time, and hell deeper than the sea, and God's wrath against sin mightier than its waves, and fiercer than the fires of Sodom; and can these be stayed? Yes, yes, since Christ received all this wrath into His own soul, and there exhausted it,[6]

[1] Gen., xix. 23, 24. [2] Ex., xv. 8.
[3] Joshua, iii. 15–17. [4] Joshua, x. 12, 13.
[5] 2 Kings, xx. 1–11. [6] Is., liii. 6; John, xix. 30.

even these stand still at the cry of the weakest sinner praying in faith to Jesus Christ, or in Christ's name.[1] And if a little child even, do but trust in Him, he may walk through the valley of the shadow of death, singing as he goes this cheerful song of defiance, O Death, where is thy sting? O Grave, where is thy victory?[2] For, since the Messiah was cut off, but not for Himself, He hath made an end of sin, and brought in everlasting righteousness; the Law is satisfied, and the head of the old Serpent bruised.[3]

Then let burdened sinners be of good heart and come to Jesus Christ. Let them cry for mercy where they will, their faith may be sure that Jesus Christ is "standing still" just before them, looking kindly on them, and ready to give them His blessing. He passed that way that Bartimeus might cry to Him, and He came on earth that we might all cry to Him for mercy. Our crying is the fruit of His coming, not its cause. He came of His own grace, and we pray because of our need. But

[1] Mark, ix. 23; Rom., viii. 31–39.
[2] Ps. xxiii. 4; 1 Cor., xv. 55. [3] Dan., ix. 24, 26; Gen., iii. 15

we would have sat for ever voiceless and despairing in our blindness, if His coming had not filled our hearts with hope, and our mouths with supplications.

The three evangelists united in saying that "Jesus stood still," but now their expressions differ. Each one sounds a note which the others do not wake, and together they make a noble harmony. Do not fail to notice the advantage of comparing Scripture with Scripture. This is one of the most beautiful instances I have found. Matthew says, "He called;" Mark, "He commanded him to be called;" and Luke, "He commanded him to be brought unto Him." There you have the three great steps in a sinner's effectual calling illustrated. Bartimeus was called, Sovereignly, by the voice of Christ; Instrumentally, by the voice of men; and Efficiently, by the helping hands which guided his willing steps to Jesus. So we may look upon his call, and the gracious call of every sinner who becomes a saint, in its divine Origin, its gentle Instruments, and its effectual Aids.

I. "He called." Our vocation is of God. He

hath called us out of darkness into His marvellous light.[1] The God of all grace hath called us unto His eternal glory by Christ Jesus.[2] Our calling is a holy calling, a high calling, a heavenly calling.[3] Its source is divine grace, its rule the divine purpose, and it is the fruit of election. We are chosen in eternity and called in time.[4]

"He called." This word of Matthew contains, as in the seed, the expressions of Mark and Luke. All the agencies, by which the soul is persuaded and enabled to embrace Jesus Christ freely offered to us in the gospel, are hidden in this, His loving call, as the leaves and flowers and golden fruit are all folded in the germ. Many Providences, many Scriptures, many ordinances, many movements of the Spirit may lay hold on a soul to draw it to Christ; but they are all so many threads which Christ holds in His own hand. They have all their power from His drawing.

Then let us use this truth for holy fear. If you resist the appeals of God's ministers, you

[1] 1 Pet., ii. 9. [2] 1 Pet., v. 10. [3] 2 Tim., i. 9; Phil., iii. 4; Heb., iii. 1. [4] Gal., i. 15; Rom., viii. 30; 2 Tim., i. 9, 10.

resist God. If you despise God's Providences, you despise Him. If you stifle the alarms of conscience, you are silencing the Voice from heaven, which may speak to you no more till it speak in the thunders of the Judgment. Oh, see that ye refuse not Him that speaketh from heaven. He that despised Moses' law died without mercy. And a sorer punishment—sorer than a death, sure, bloody and merciless, is in reserve for all who turn away from Him that speaketh from heaven. For our God is a consuming fire.[1]

Let us also use this truth for holy encouragement. Is it indeed Christ's voice that speaks by sacraments and Sabbaths and gospel ministers? Then let faith cry, The voice of my Beloved![2] and open the door, and He shall come in and sup with us and we with Him.[3] We shall feed upon the promises, and His fruit shall be sweet to our taste.[4] Our hearts shall burn within us,[5] our sorrows be comforted, our burdens lightened, our graces revived. A bundle of myrrh shall He be to

[1] Heb., x. 28, 29; xii. 25, 29. [2] Song, ii. 8.
[3] Rev., iii. 20. [4] Song, ii. 3. [5] Luke, xxiv. 32.

us, and a cluster of camphire from the vineyards of En-gedi.[1]

"He called." In Jesus Christ we behold the best of preachers,—the divine Exemplar after whom all should copy.

While He lived on earth He called to men every where, saying, If any man thirst let him come unto me and drink.[2] In His zeal to proclaim the glad tidings of salvation through faith in His name, any spot became a pulpit, any lost sinner a sufficient audience. He preached indeed in the Temple frequently, and in the synagogues habitually, all over the land;[3] but also in the street, on the mountain, and on the strand;[4] as He walked by the way or sat at meals;[5] when the multitude broke in upon His quiet retreat in the country, which He had sought with His disciples, for a little needful rest,[6] or when the timid inquirer came to Him by night,[7] or the guilty woman of Samaria questioned Him as He sat in weariness, at noon, on Jacobs's well;[8] wheth-

[1] Song, i. 14. [2] John, vii. 37. [3] Luke, xix. 47; iv. 16, 44.
[4] Luke, xiii. 26; Mat., v. 1; Luke, xiii. 1, 2.
[5] Luke, xxiv. 15, 27; Luke, xiv. [6] Mark, vi. 31–34.
[7] John, iii. 1, 2. [8] John, iv. 6.

er the great ones of Church and State were arrayed before Him, or the poor and the diseased, the publican and the abhorred outcast besought His mercy.[1] All moved His pity. None were sent empty away. Never was He so exhausted that He could not give rest to the heavy-laden. Thirsting Himself, He gave to others the cup of living water.[2] On his way to the Cross, condemned, forsaken, scourged and bleeding, He tenderly addressed the mourning daughters of Jerusalem, and in the very anguish of death, He gave eternal life to the penitent robber by whom He had just been reviled.[3]

Such a Preacher was Christ: yet it was expedient for us that He should go away. The purposed ends of His personal ministry on earth were accomplished, and it was needful that He should leave the world and go to the Father, there to prepare a place for us, that so He might come again, and receive us to Himself.[4] But meantime, the preaching of the gospel was not to cease.

[1] Mat., xxiii.; Luke, vii. 36–50; xv. [2] John, iv. 10.
[3] Luke, xxiii. 28, 40–43, with Mat., xxvii. 44.
[4] John, xiv. 2, 3; xvi. 7, 28.

II. "He commanded him to be called." The Lord gave the word; great was the company of them that published it.[1] He did not leave Himself without a witness, nor His people without a comforter.[2] When He ascended up on high, He led captivity captive, and gave gifts unto men.[3] Chiefest Gift, Chiefest Witness and Chiefest Comforter was the Holy Ghost. But besides Him, and under His ministration, He gave some, apostles; and some, prophets; and some, pastors and teachers; for the perfecting of the saints, for the work of the ministry, for the edifying of the body of Christ.[4]

God having reconciled the world unto Himself by Jesus Christ, hath given to us the ministry of reconciliation, so that we are ambassadors for Christ, as though God did beseech you by us; we pray you in Christ's stead be ye reconciled to God.[5] The divine wisdom is clearly seen in this. The treasure is in earthen vessels that the excellency of the power may be of God, and not of us.[6] If

[1] Ps. lxviii. 11. [2] Acts, i. 8; John, xiv. 16–18. [3] Eph., iv. 8.
[4] Eph., iv. 11, 12. [5] 2 Cor., v. 18–20. [6] 2 Cor., iv. 7.

under the music and thunder of angelic voices the soul was converted, while the Sabbath air was fragrant with heavenly odors and quivering with bright wings, our foolish hearts, all enravished with the splendor of the vision, and thrilling still to the celestial eloquence, would ascribe to these flaming ministers the glory, saying, By *their* might, by their power, and *not* by the Spirit of the Lord![1] But when the worm Jacob threshes the mountains,[2] the Spirit is honored, and Christ is honored, and men and angels cry together, Not unto us, O Lord, not unto us, but unto Thy name give glory, for Thy mercy, and for Thy truth's sake.[3]

And so it must be. God cannot give His glory to another.[4] The saved must all be saved by grace, and own it too.[5] The shout of Grace! Grace! shall be heard over every stone in the Heavenly Temple.[6]

So too, do the preachers of the gospel stand before the people as trophies of the grace they proclaim. Therefore the preaching comes

[1] Zech., iv. 6. [2] Isa., xli. 14, 15. [3] Ps. cxv. 1.
[4] Is., xlii. 8. [5] 2 Tim., i. 9. [6] Zech., iv. 7

with the power and tenderness of experience. "I preached," says Bunyan, "what I felt, what I smartingly did feel, even that under which my poor soul did groan and tremble to astonishment. Indeed, I have been as one sent to them from the dead. I went myself in chains, to preach to them in chains; and carried in my own conscience that fire I persuaded them to beware of. I can truly say, and that without dissembling, that when I have been to preach, I have gone full of guilt and terror, even to the pulpit door, and there it hath been taken off, and I have been at liberty in my mind until I have done my work."[1] Oh, who cannot imagine the tenderness, the inflamed earnestness and heart-melting pathos with which he must then have preached!

If we "call" because Christ has "commanded," then are we servants of Christ, servants of the Church for His sake, and servants of the gospel. Therefore must we preach not ourselves, but Christ Jesus our Lord.[2] As our calling sinners grows out of His calling

[1] Grace Abounding. [2] 2 Cor., iv. 5.

them, our great business is to repeat, expound and enforce His teachings. His Word is to be the substance of our preaching,[1] His Spirit our Helper,[2] Himself our Exemplar.[3] Then will He stand by us.[4] When we speak from His mouth, He will speak by our mouths. Through our voice of weakness will sound His voice of power. When in heathen lands we can but stammer brokenly, in a half-learned language, the story of the Cross, He will be there, translating to the longing heart the glad tidings. When we appear *for* Him, He appears *in* us.

Let him that heareth, say, Come![5] Then all the called may themselves become callers. Some are especially chosen and ordained to this work, but every saint may have a share in it. O soul, once sick unto death, hast thou found the great Physician? Run quickly to thy dying neighbors, and tell them what He has done for thee. Ah! how canst thou help it? If thou canst hold thy tongue from pub-

[1] 2 Tim., iv. 1, 2. [2] Acts, ii. 4; Eph., vi. 19.
[3] 1 Cor., xi. 1; 1 John, ii. 6. [4] Mat., xxviii. 20.
[5] Rev., xxii. 17.

lishing His fame, thou deservest that it should stiffen in eternal silence for its base selfishness and ingratitude!

III. And now what a word of good cheer the third evangelist speaks—"He commanded him to be brought unto Him!" Admire the Lord's grace to the blind man. He will not leave him to grope his dark way alone. Some shall lead him by the hand. In whatever way, he shall have all the aid he needs to come into the Saviour's very presence.

Blessed thought! that we who are but men, may have some share in this dear work of guiding blind souls to Jesus. There is no dignity like it on this side of heaven; no bliss like it to be tasted on earth. It is worth living for, worth dying for, to guide one lost sinner to his Redeemer.

But here I rather choose to think of the higher than human aid, which Christ sends with His word to the souls of His chosen. The energy of Almighty power accompanies the preaching of the truth.[1] The *Spirit* and the Bride say, Come![2] There is your hope

[1] Eph., i. 17–20. [2] Rev., xxii. 17.

and our consolation. While we call from our pulpits, Christ calls from heaven, and the Spirit calls in your very hearts. At the word of Christ, we *tell* you of your blindness; only the Spirit can *convince* you of your blindness.[1] We tell you of Christ; only the Spirit can take of the things of Christ, and show them to you.[2] He alone can shine into your hearts to give the light of the knowledge of the glory of God in the face of Christ.[3] We can prophesy to the dry bones in the Valley of Vision; only He can clothe them with flesh and fill them with life, till they shall rise and go forth a great army.[4] When bidden, we can stretch out the rod over the sea; only He can make it a rod of might, and send the strong wind which shall change the sea to dry land.[5] But all these this mighty Spirit can do, and will do, at the will of Christ, for the word of Christ.

Therefore we are of good courage. We are weak, but our Helper is strong. We take the word of Jesus, and while it seems but a word

[1] John, xvi. 8, margin. [2] John, xvi. 15. [3] 2 Cor., iv. 6.
[4] Ezek., xxxvii. 1–10. [5] Ex., xiv. 16, 21.

from human lips, the Spirit makes it the power of God for salvation.[1] It suddenly becomes a two-edged sword, quick and powerful, in the hands of Omnipotence. It pierces to the dividing asunder of soul and spirit, and of the joints and marrow—almighty to accomplish the whole sovereign will of Christ.[2]

Sinner, I charge you, remember the dreadful sanction Christ puts on the preaching of His ambassadors in those words: He that despiseth you, despiseth Me, and he that despiseth Me, despiseth Him that sent Me.[3] It is Heavenly Wisdom that now cries, Turn you at my reproof; behold I will pour out my Spirit unto you. I will make known my words unto you.[4] Beware, then, lest one day you hear that awful voice, Because I have called, and ye have refused; I have stretched out my hand, and no man regarded; but ye have set at nought all my counsel, and would none of my reproof; I also will laugh at your calamity; I will mock when your fear cometh; when your fear cometh as desolation,

[1] Rom., i., 16. [2] Heb., iv. 12; Is., lv. 11.
[3] Luke, x. 16 [4] Prov., i. 23.

and your destruction as a whirlwind; when distress and anguish cometh upon you! Then shall they call upon me, but I will not answer; they shall seek me early, but they shall not find me![1]

O Christ, I have preached the preaching Thou hast bidden me. Honor Thine own word, and send thine effectual aids!

O Spirit of Jesus, glorify the truth in Jesus. Display Thine Almighty power, and lead these poor sinners to Jesus Christ!

[1] Prov., i. 24–28.

VI.

"And they call the blind man, saying unto him, Be of good comfort; rise; He calleth thee. And he, casting away his garment, rose and came to Jesus."

WHAT a lively picture of gospel preaching! The seeing hasten to the sightless and bid them come to Jesus Christ. Men whose eyes have seen the Lord, and whose ears have heard His gracious words, go at His command, to souls sitting in the region and shadow of death,[1] and there proclaim aloud these joyful tidings.

The analogy would be perfect, if those who were sent to Bartimeus had themselves been blind, until their eyes had been opened by Christ. And who can say that it was not so with some of them? Christ had healed many blind men, and it is far from improbable that some of them followed Him ever after, wait-

[1] Mat., iv. 16.

ing to be sent on these joyful errands of grace.

Then with what generous indignation must they have heard the cruel rebukes of the multitude! O gospel preachers, both lay and clerical—all who in public or in private, in the pulpit or by the way-side, have any thing to tell to others of Christ's gracious dealings with your souls, remember the wormwood and the gall[1] of your lost estate, and let a righteous anger burn against the world, the flesh and the devil, against priest and pharisee, and every ungodly Church and professor, who would silence the cries of convicted souls. Think of the woes of perishing sinners, and let an honest zeal for their deliverance from ruin kindle your heart and tongue against all the agencies of hell, however disguised, baptized or consecrated, who would drive even the meanest sinners—publicans and harlots, from Jesus Christ. Feel as men once rescued from a wreck would feel, if they saw, upon a stormy sea, "swimmers in their agony" weakly grasping the icy shore, only to be inhumanly thrust back into the wintry waves.

[1] Lam., iii. 19.

Then too, with what alarmed sympathy would these men, once blind, now seeing, have regarded Bartimeus, if he had wavered in his earnestness after Christ! What would they not have done to have roused him again to his importunity? O gospel preachers, be it so with you. Let your hearts melt with concern for timid souls turning away from Christ through discouragement. Oh, that we could all say with Paul, My little children, of whom I travail in birth again, till Christ be formed in you.[1] Oh that all ministers and all Christians felt such anguish of love for halting souls.

And with what alacrity would these messengers of Christ have hastened to bear His words of welcome to the blind man! Joy beyond expression would have inspired them. I have heard of a caravan which had lost its way in the desert. For days they could find no water. The suffering was sore, and many were perishing. Men were out in all directions searching for the water that was to be, indeed, water of life. At last, faint and ready

[1] Gal., iv. 19.

to die, one man lighted on a spring. Cool and clear the stream gushed from the rock. Almost frantic with thirst, he rushed forward and drank, drank. Oh how deep was the bliss of that draught! Is it strange that for one moment he thought only of himself? But suddenly the perishing multitude came before his mind, and he leaped up, and ran shouting, "Water! water! Enough for all! Come and drink!" And so from rank to rank of that scattered host he sped, until he had told them all, and was himself thirsty again. But when he saw the eager crowds rushing to the fountain, when he beheld the refreshment and gladness of all hearts and faces, and then stooped once more himself to drink the liberal stream, was not his second draught full of deeper bliss than even the first? Had he ever tasted such water as that? O blessed souls who have drank of the river of life, lift up your voice upon the mountains, and let your feet be swift upon the plains, publishing the good tidings of salvation.[1]

This brings to view the joyfulness of the

[1] Isa., lii. 7.

gospel. It is *not* a message of gloom, a thing to be whispered in darkness as a dreadful secret. We dishonor the gospel when we would recommend it by a melancholy visage. We have not entered into its spirit, if, when we would press its claims upon a friend, we go stealthily aside, and hang our heads, and use lugubrious speech, and seem like doleful culprits at the confessional, instead of free citizens of the Kingdom, rejoicing in our coming inheritance of inconceivable glory. When the hypocrites in Isaiah's time would keep a fast, they bowed their heads as a bulrush, and spread sackcloth and ashes under them.[1] And in Christ's day, they were of a sad countenance, and disfigured their faces; but Christ rebuked this, and required His disciples rather to wash their faces, and anoint their heads, that even in keeping a fast, they might lack none of the usual tokens of cheerfulness.[2]

Oh, the gospel *is* joyful! It found the race cowering in despair by the forbidden tree, under the threatened vengeance of Jehovah; and it will not leave them, till the last of the

[1] Isa., lviii. 5. [2] Mat., vi. 16, 17.

chosen seed are exulting in eternal song before their Father's Throne. When it first visited our world, the earth was groaning and travailing in the bondage of corruption. But the Redeemer shall one day break these chains, and introduce the burdened creation into the glorious liberty of the children of God. It is already waiting for their manifestation, and leaning forward in eager hope of its own deliverance.[1]

The gospel gloomy! It is an anthem from the harps of heaven, the music of the River of Life washing its shores on high, and pouring in cascades upon the earth. Not so cheerful was the song of the morning stars, nor the shout of the sons of God so joyful.[2] Gushing from the fountains of eternal harmony, it was first heard on earth in a low tone of solemn gladness, uttered in Eden, by the Lord God Himself.[3] This gave the key-note of the gospel song. Patriarchs caught it up, and taught it to the generations following. It breathed from the harp of Psalmists, and rang like a clarion from tower and mountain-top, as pro-

[1] Rom., viii. 19–23. [2] Job, xxxviii. 7. [3] Gen., iii. 15.

phets proclaimed the year of jubilee. Fresh notes from heaven have enriched the harmony, as the Lord of Hosts and His angels have revealed new promises, and called on the suffering children of Zion to be joyful in their King.[1] From bondage and exile, from dens and caves, from bloody fields and fiery stakes and peaceful death-beds have they answered, in tones which have cheered the disconsolate, and made oppressors shake upon their thrones; while sun and moon and all the stars of light, stormy wind fulfilling His word, the roaring sea and the fulness thereof, mountains and hills, fruitful fields and all the trees of the wood have rejoiced before the Lord, and the coming of His Anointed, for the redemption of His people, and the glory of His holy Name.[2]

The gospel gloomy! If the best right, and the only right to be glad on earth, with the assured prospect of eternal blessedness in heaven; if songs in the night[3] and stars of promise; if the light of morning with its

[1] Ps. cxlix. 2. [2] Ps. xcviii. 11–13; cxlviii. 3, 8.
[3] Job, xxxv. 10.

fragrant breath and singing birds; if health for the sick, return for the banished, pardon for the doomed, and life for the dying; if love, joy, peace, hope; if harp and crown and waving palm, and the everlasting vision of the Redeemer's glory be gloomy, *then* is the gospel gloomy!

Such is the spirit of the tidings these messengers bring to Bartimeus, in this, his second gospel sermon. The first told him simply that Jesus was passing by. Now he hears these heart-reviving words, "Be of good comfort; rise; He calleth thee."

"Be of good comfort." On thy long night, without moon or star, or even a dim candle in thy dwelling, the Day-star is dawning.[1] Thine eyes have never been used but for weeping; they seemed only made for tears. But now they shall serve thee for seeing. Thou shalt look upon earth and sky and all dear faces and even Christ thy Saviour. Rejoice, too, for thy poverty and beggary are ended. Thou shalt work with thy hands, and eat the bread of thine own honest toil. Be of good

[1] Luke, i. 78; Rev., xxii. 16.

heart. With Jesus for thy physician, thou needst not fear. He never casts any away, and He never fails. At His touch, how have we seen the blind gaze, the dumb sing, the lame cast away their crutches, and leap for joy, and even the dead awake and live![1]

Sinners, poor, wretched and blind, but crying for the Saviour, be not disconsolate. "Be of good comfort." After *your* night of weeping, your morning of joy has come.[2] On your hearts the Day-star is rising.[3] Come to Jesus, and roam and grope and beg no more. Do not fear to come. Oh He is gracious! Oh He is mighty! His blood cleanseth from all sin.[4] He is able to save to the uttermost.[5] This is the work in which His soul delighteth. None can measure His love. It is stronger than death, even the death of the Cross. And the satisfaction He desires for all the travail of His soul, is just to pardon and cleanse guilty sinners.[7] "Be of good comfort" then, and come to Jesus Christ.

"Rise!" say the preachers to Bartimeus, and

[1] Mat., xi. 5. [2] Ps. xxx. 5. [3] 2 Pet., i. 19. [4] John, i. 7. [5] Heb., vii. 25. [6] Eph., iii. 19. [7] Is., liii. 10, 11.

so we cry. There is salvation for the sinner, none for the sluggard. There is pardon for all sin, except not coming to Jesus.[1] Whether from hatred, doubt, or indifference, it is the same, if you will not rise and come, you perish. Laziness is a slow devil. He looks easy, and sometimes amiable. But none are more obstinate, and few have carried more to hell than he. Not to receive Christ is to reject Him. Not to love Him is to hate Him and be Anathema.[2] How often would I have gathered you, says Christ, as He weeps over the doom of Jerusalem, but ye would not![3] Ah, that is the secret of damnation—Ye *would* not come unto me that ye might have life. Rise, then, ye unpardoned. Away with your fears and doubts. They are unreasonable and wicked. Break off your indifference. It is a noiseless chain, indeed, but be not deceived; the chain that does not clank is the tightest. Let me take the trumpet of the Holy Ghost, and may He fill it with a sound that shall pierce your heart;—Awake thou that sleepest,

[1] John, vi. 37, with v. 40. [2] 1 Cor., xvi. 22.
[3] Mat., xxiii. 37.

and arise from the dead, and Christ shall give thee light![1]

"He calleth thee." What more canst thou want, Bartimeus? If He *calls* thee, He will cure thee. If *He* calls, who can forbid? His call would clear a way for thee through all this multitude, if they should oppose. All the devils in hell could not keep thee back, poor, sightless, helpless man, if thy Saviour calls thee.

Thy call is thy warrant. The call of Christ is warrant enough for any sinner. He may use it against the Law and Satan and his own evil conscience. For example, Satan comes to him and says,

"What, wretch! art thou going to Christ?"

"Aye, that I am, with all my heart."

"But will He receive thee?"

"Aye, that He will, with all His heart."

"Truly, thou art a brave talker! Who taught thee this lofty speech?"

"Nay, my speech is lowly, and I learned it of my Lord."

"But where is thy warrant? None can go to Christ without a warrant."

[1] Eph., v. 14.

"He calleth me—be *that* my warrant!"

"But where is thy fitness?" says Satan, shifting his ground.

"Be my warrant my fitness—He calleth me," answers the sinner keeping his ground, his only ground.

"But listen, soul! Thou art going before a King. He cannot look upon iniquity,"[1] (for you see Satan can quote Scripture,) "and thou art but a mass of iniquity;" (here the devil affects a great horror of it, to fill the sinner with fear.) "The heavens are not clean in His sight;[2] how then shall thy filthiness appear before Him? Look at thy rags, if thy blind eyes will let thee, and say, what a dress is this to take into His presence!"

"It is all true," says the contrite sinner, "still I will go, for He calleth me. I will bind this call about me and it shall be my dress, till He give me another. I will hold up this call, written with His own hand, and signed with His own name, and sealed with His own blood, and it shall be my defence and plea. Miserable and unworthy as I am, and deserv-

[1] Hab., i. 13. [2] Job, xv. 15.

ing, I know, to die, with this I have boldness and access with confidence,[1] saying only, like little Samuel, Here am I, for Thou didst call me!"[2]

Bartimeus needed no more. "Casting away his garment, he rose and came to Jesus." It could not be otherwise. True earnestness does not wait. Conscious wretchedness in the presence of a trusted Saviour cannot delay. Only half-convictions can procrastinate. Sinners who hang back and yet look forward, longing and tarrying, hearing a thousand exhortations but waiting for one more, have either shallow views of sin or low views of Christ. I pray you take heed of that; there is your trouble,—shallow views of sin or low views of Christ. Either you do not see your need of such a Saviour, or you do not see Him to be the Saviour you need. If you knew what a sinner you are, and what a Saviour He is, you would go to Him at once and be saved.

"A full conviction of sin," says John Owen,[3] "is a great and shaking surprisal unto a guilty soul." And without such surprisals men will

[1] Eph., iii. 12. [2] 1 Sam., iii. 6. [3] On Heb. vi. 18.

die in their carnal security. Therefore though the gospel is indeed a message of gladness, its preachers must often preach heavy and bitter things. The Old Testament ends with the word "Curse," while the New begins with this announcement, "The book of the generation of Jesus Christ." But until this sound of an avenging Law has rung dreadfully in the sinner's ears, little will he care for the glad tidings of the gospel.

Would to God our message might ever sound in music and not in thunder—that we might stand evermore on the green top of sunlit Gerizim, and never again on the stormy height of gloomy Ebal[1]—that our doctrine might drop as the rain, and our speech distil as the dew, as the small rain upon the tender herb, and as the showers upon the grass![2] But what care they for refuge who have not heard of wrath? for Calvary, who have never trembled under the blaze and roar of Sinai? for pardon, who are not convinced of sin? for the treasures hid in Christ, who say, I am rich and increased with goods, and have need of

[1] Deut., xi. 29. [2] Deut., xxxii. 2.

nothing; and know not, alas! that they are wretched and miserable, and poor, and blind, and naked![1]

If our hearers were all like Bartimeus, our message might always begin, "Be of good comfort." If men felt their burdens, we would gently say, Come unto me, all ye that labor and are heavy laden, and I will give you rest.[2] If they were conscious of their thirst, how joyfully would we cry, Ho, every one that thirsteth, come ye to the waters![3] If they were already cut to the heart with sharp convictions, and were crying to us, Sirs, what must we do to be saved? most gladly would we answer, Believe on the Lord Jesus Christ, and ye *shall* be saved.[4]

The gospel *is* joyful, though it has one note of terror—He that believeth not shall be damned.[5] It announces that there is no need of damnation. We may all be saved, if we will but believe. It does not create our condemnation,[6] we are condemned already.[7] It finds us in chains and tells us how we may escape.

[1] Rev., iii. 17. [2] Mat., xi. 28. [3] Isa., lv. 1.
[4] Acts, xvi. 29–31. [5] Mark, xvi. 16. [6] John, iii. 17.
[7] John, iii. 18.

Am I not still the bearer of glad tidings, if I burst into the cell of the doomed man and cry, Here is your pardon! Come out at once, and you shall live! even if, as I see him contentedly hugging his chain, or sinking back into his stupid sleep, I seize him with rough kindness, and cry out to him with an energy of love that seems like fierceness, Rise and flee, or you perish! All who are found within these walls, when the bell of doom begins to toll, must die!

The ancient heathen had this saying; "The feet of the avenging deities are shod with wool." Shod with wool! Yes, they crept with noiseless steps, that the touch that aroused, might be the blow that destroyed. It is not so with our merciful God. He sounds an alarm that we may seek a refuge. His thunder rolls along the distant horizon, that we may take in sail and be ready for the storm, the storm which would have burst upon us no less surely, without this gracious warning.

As Bartimeus rose to hasten to Jesus, he "cast away his garment," his loose upper robe. He would suffer no hindrance. He may have thrown it aside unconsciously, but it was the action of nature—nature in earnest for some great end.

Let us take the lesson. If we would win Christ, we must lay aside every weight, and the sin which so easily besets us[1]—the sin we have daily wrapped about us like our garment. We must forget those things which are behind, and reach forth unto those things which are before.[2] Hearken, O daughter, and consider, and incline thine ear; forget also thine own people and thy father's house. So shall the King greatly desire thy beauty; for He is thy Lord, and worship thou Him.[3]

Cain sacrificed unto the Lord, but he could not cast off his envy, and it soon constrained him to murder.[4] Balaam sighed for the death of the righteous; but when he saw the wages of unrighteousness, they seemed so goodly a garment, that he drew it around him, and died a very different death indeed—slain by the avenging sword of Israel, and mingling his blood with the blood of those he had se-

[1] Heb., xii. 1. [2] Phil., iii. 13. [3] Ps. xlv. 10, 11.
[4] Gen., iv. 3, 5, 8.

duced into licentiousness and idolatry.[1] Felix trembled as Paul preached; but procrastination was so wrapped about him that he could not cast it off, and so he never came to Christ.[2] When Herod heard John the Baptist, he did many things, and heard him gladly; yet when the stern prophet put forth his hand to tear away the robe of lust, whose clinging poison was eating into his soul, he bound him in prison and murdered him, and died, at length, in exile and shame.[3] The young Ruler came even running to Christ, such was his eagerness for salvation; but a searching word about his possessions suddenly stopped him. He hesitated, he yearned for the blessing of eternal life. He was so guileless, so full of virtue, so ingenuous, so warm in his aspirations for immortal purity and blessedness. He looked upon Jesus with longing; Jesus looked upon him with love. Is it too much to believe that they both wept? But ah! that cloth of gold in which he had arrayed himself, and which he wore in his high station with such grace

1 Num., xxiii. 10; 2 Pet., ii. 15; Num., xxxi. 8, 16.
2 Acts, xxiv. 25.
3 Mark, vi. 17, 20, 27.

and pride—that jewelled robe seemed too precious to rend and scatter to the poor; so he drew it slowly around him, and went sorrowfully away, and it became, I fear, his poor soul's winding-sheet![1] Ananias and Sapphira professed the faith of Christ, joined the Church, and even made a great sacrifice of their possessions for it; but unable to cast off the garment of lying ostentation, God touched it with His wrath, and consumed them.[2] Judas was numbered with the twelve apostles, and obtained part of their ministry; but he still wore the secret robe of avarice, and it grew to his very flesh, and ate into his heart as a canker, and when his heart was gone, he betrayed his Master, and hurried to perdition.[3]

How do these cases search and condemn many professors of religion! Cain shows that professed worshippers of God may perish; Balaam and Felix, that holy aspirations and fearful convictions may yet end in destruction; Herod, that those who hear joyfully the

[1] Mark, x. 17–22. [2] Acts, v. 1–11.
[3] Acts, i. 17; John, xii. 6; Mat., xxvi. 14–16, 47–49; xxvii. 5.

most faithful preaching and go far in their obedience, may yet be lost. The young man whom Jesus loved proves the utter insufficiency of human virtue without the grace of God. Ah, more; how much it is to be feared that that same word about the possessions spoken to many in this day, who are "running" most complacently in their profession, would give them a check from which they would never recover. And as to the sin of Ananias and Sapphira, it would seem that many modern Church members think that the essence of the sin was in selling the land at all, and laying any part of the price at the Apostles' feet! Oh, how should they be afraid, who are content that souls now in hell should have surpassed all *their* proofs of love to Christ and His poor! Lastly, the perdition of the traitor rings an alarm-bell in the ears, not only of all professors, but all ministers, crying out that they, who have preached the gospel to others, may themselves be cast away.[1]

There is yet one garment, which more than

[1] 1 Cor., ix. 27.

all others men hug about them, and that is Self-righteousness. It is a miserable and filthy affair, a thing of patch-work and rags.[1] But the blind sinner thinks it fair and comely. He draws it about him in pride, and his soul has comfort.

Some men toil all their lives to make it large and clean and beautiful, and to set it richly with gems of virtue and good works. Paul was a diligent worker at this, and for a while he thought himself very successful, and used to survey himself in the glass of the law with great complacency. He counts over to us seven fair colors that were woven into it, making it, in his estimation, like a rainbow for beauty;—If any other man thinketh he hath whereof he might trust in the flesh, I more; circumcised the eighth day, of the stock of Israel, of the tribe of Benjamin, an Hebrew of the Hebrews; as touching the law, a Pharisee; concerning zeal, persecuting the Church; touching the righteousness which is in the law, blameless![2] On all these he looked with great satisfaction, little knowing how blind he

[1] Is., lxiv. 6.

[2] Phil., iii. 4–6.

was, nor what a poor, unsightly wretch in the eyes of God. But when the great light from heaven shone upon him, and God opened his eyes,[1] he saw that he was vile, and had no righteousness at all.[2] He poured nothing but contempt on the glory of his old pride.[3] As he grew older he seemed to delight to stain it more and more.[4] At last, many years after, he wrote a letter to his son Timothy, and confessed that all that time he was a blasphemer, and a persecutor and injurious, and the chief of sinners.[5]

This garment must always be renounced when a sinner would come to Jesus Christ. But it is very hard to do. The old ploughman was right when he told Hervey that it was harder to get rid of righteous self than of sinful self. Hervey thought it a very ridiculous speech at the time, for he knew little of grace then; but afterwards he learned in the school of Christ that it was so indeed.

Some remainders, of it, however,—some shreds and patches, hang about all saints on

[1] Acts, ix. 1–18. [2] Phil., iii. 3. [3] Phil., iii. 7–9.
[4] 1 Cor., xv. 9, with Eph., iii. 8, and 1 Tim., i. 15.
[5] 1 Tim., i. 13, 15, 16.

earth. And what is very marvellous, even after they have seen and abhorred its filthiness, if God would suffer, they would all fall to, and weave these rags together again, and think them comely, and wear them in pride!

Job, who was one of the best of men, was once found doing too much of this, (as you may see in the twenty-ninth and thirty-first chapters,) when God suddenly gave him a sight of himself in the mirror of infinite majesty and sovereignty,[1] and the sight so overwhelmed him that he exclaimed, I am vile.[2] Once more God flashed the light of that terrible mirror upon him,[3] for He meant to make thorough work, and Job cried out, I have heard of Thee by the hearing of the ear; but now mine eye seeth Thee; wherefore I abhor myself, and repent in dust and ashes.[4]

Oh that God may give us all grace to cast this wretched garment away, tearing it and stamping it in the dust, that we may win

[1] Job, chapters xxxviii., xxxix. and xl. 1, 2.
[2] Job, xl. 3. [3] Job, xl. 6–24, and chapter xli.
[4] Job, xlii. 5, 6.

Christ, and be found in Him, not having our own righteousness, which is of the law, but that which is through the faith of Christ, the righteousness which is of God by faith![1]

[1] Phil., iii. 8, 9.

VII.

"And Jesus answered and said unto him, What wilt thou that I should do unto thee? The blind man said unto Him, Lord that I might receive my sight!"

BARTIMEUS is at length at the feet of Jesus. He cannot see Him yet, but he feels it good to be there—there in the dust, there in darkness.

And who ever found it otherwise? Oh, what sorrows have been brought to the Saviour's feet—shame, disappointment, bereavement, sickness of heart and flesh, the stings of remorse, the inward burning of divine wrath, the pains of utter despair! But who that ever came in wretchedness did not here find blessedness?

I do not mean now the blessedness of the final and great relief, when heavenly light has streamed through all the broken heart and healed it; but the blessedness, simply, of having come to Jesus, the blessedness of being consciously near Him.

All coming to Christ is good. While only the Law works, the sinner only suffers. The cliffs of Sinai are falling. Heavy bolts from the thick darkness where God is, break the heart.[1] But the Gospel gives peace. We joy in God through our Lord Jesus Christ by whom we have now received the atonement.[2] The sun brightens and warms all who look upon it, though they come from cold, foul caverns. And Christ is a Sun. He gives grace and glory to the most miserable of sinners and His bitterest enemies, if they look to Him in faith.[3] If the bruised and aching heart be brought within the shining of the Cross, its beams will glide into it, and fill it with secret refreshments. There is comfort in resolving to flee to Christ, comfort in fleeing, comfort in falling at His feet. I trow Bartimeus was never so truly happy before, and yet he is still a beggar, lying in unrelieved blindness in the dust at the feet of Jesus of Nazareth.

The feet of Jesus! There the sinner finds

[1] Rom., vii. 7–13. [2] Rom., v. 11.
[3] Ps. lxxxiv. 11, with Mal., iv. 2.

all that the needs of his own soul, all that the demands of the Law, all that the Perfections of God require. There he sees the Antetype of all the types, the Substance of all the shadows, the Fulfilment of all the promises. There his guilt is pardoned, his foulness cleansed, his person accepted. For there is at once the Priest and the Sacrifice, the blood of sprinkling and the way into the Holiest of all.[1] There is the true Mercy-seat and the Shekinah,—the visible glory of the Divine presence between the cherubim.[2] There *God* is manifest in the *flesh*.[3]

At the feet of Jesus none need be afraid. This beggar drew "near." In Him we have boldness and access with confidence through the faith of Him.[4] It is impossible to press too near to Christ. In the Song the Spouse is seen coming up from the wilderness leaning upon her Beloved.[5] Like John at the Supper we may rest upon His very breast.[6] The good Shepherd loves to see His sheep lying near

[1] Heb., ix. 11–14; x. 19–22.
[2] Ex., xxv. 22.
[3] 1 Tim., iii. 16.
[4] Eph., iii. 12.
[5] Song, viii. 5.
[6] John, xiii. 23.

His feet, and when the lambs are weary He carries them in His bosom.[1]

In the days of His flesh His invitation was evermore, Come unto me![2] The exiled leper heard, and burst through all to come into His presence and fall at His feet.[3] The multitudes heard, and again and again did they "throng" Him, "press" upon Him.[4]

But so far was He from being offended, that, though they were poor and covered with disease, loathsome to sight and touch, He healed them all.[5] Publicans and sinners heard, and even while He and His disciples sat at meat, they came and sat with them.[6] So freely did He receive them and mingle with them, that He was sneeringly called, The Friend of publicans and sinners.[7] They meant it for shame, but He took it for glory. The ruined outcast heard—ah! who can ever forget that tender scene of grace, in which He so vindicates and blesses the polluted woman, who, in the bitterness of her contrition, came unbidden to the feast of the haughty Pharisee,

[1] Is., xl. 11. [2] Mat., xi. 28; Mark, x. 14; John, vii. 37.
[3] Luke, v. 12. [4] Luke, viii. 19, 45.
[5] Mat., xii. 19. [6] Mat., ix. 10, 11. [7] Mat., xi. 19.

and regardless of surprise and contempt, began to wash His feet with her tears, and did wipe them with the hairs of her head, and kissed His feet, and anointed them with the ointment of her broken alabaster box![1] And who can cease to remember, with grateful amazement, those words by which the vilest may draw near to His heart; Whosoever shall do the will of God, the same is my brother, and my sister and mother.[2]

But do you say, Christ is no longer on earth, and we cannot go to Him thus?

He has indeed passed into the heavens, and they have received Him until the times of the restitution of all things.[3] But His tender heart went with Him. He hath an unchangeable Priesthood, and *He* is the same yesterday, to-day and for ever, still a merciful and faithful High-Priest, still touched with feeling for our infirmities.[4] When of old the children of Israel watched the high-priest on the Day of Atonement, did their comfort die when he disappeared behind the veil? Did they not

[1] Luke, vii. 36–50. [2] Mark, iii. 35. [3] Acts, iii. 21.
[4] Heb., vii. 24; xiii. 8; ii. 17; iv. 15.

remember with joy that he was there completing his great work of propitiation for their sins? that their names were graven on the breast-plate which he wore on his heart? and that while he stood before the blood-sprinkled mercy-seat, in the presence of that awful glory, covered but not stricken by it, he stood as the Representative of a freely justified people?[1] Even so Christ has entered into heaven itself, the true Holy of holies, now to appear in the presence of God for us.[2] Wherefore He is able to save them to the uttermost that come to God by Him, seeing He ever liveth to make intercession for them.[3]

Years after He had taken His seat on His Throne, when He was closing the Canon of Scripture, when all seemed finished and ready for the final seal of God's dreadful malediction against him who should add to the words of the Holy Ghost, or take from them,[4] He stretched forth His hand and held back the curse until one more invitation, full, blessed, universal, poured from His heart. The Spirit

[1] Lev., xvi. [2] Heb., ix. 24. [3] Heb., vii. 25.
[4] Rev., xxii. 18, 19.

and the Bride say, Come. And let him that heareth say, Come. And let him that is athirst come. And whosoever will, let him take the water of life freely.[1]

"And when he was come near, Jesus answered." Bartimeus now, for the first time, receives the word immediately from the lips of his Lord. He is at the Well-head of life, and as he stoops to drink, the stream gushes toward him.

It is always so. If we would commune with Christ, we must draw near to Him. If we would hear His voice, we must fall down before Him. It is only there that heaven and earth may meet in peace. Christ is the true Tabernacle of the Congregation,[2] or, as that Old Testament expression may be more literally and instructively rendered, The Tabernacle of Meeting,—the divinely appointed Meeting-place; first and chiefly where God would meet His people, and they should meet Him, and *so* meet one another. Coming from all the vast circumference of Israel, there they met and found themselves one, at that holy

[1] Rev., xxii. 17. [2] Ex., xxxiii. 7.

centre, bright with the visible glory of the Godhead and the clear types of atoning grace.

Calvary is a little hill to the eye, but it is the only spot on earth that touches heaven. The Cross is foolishness to human reason, and a stumbling-block to human righteousness;[1] but there only do Mercy and Truth meet together, and Righteousness and Peace kiss each other.[2] Jesus Christ was a man of low condition, and died a death of shame on an accursed tree; but there is salvation in no other.[3] There is no Mercy-seat in the universe but at His feet.

But, lying there, we shall not only be accepted, but shall not lack some gracious word from His lips. There the broken heart shall hear its best music—a still small voice,[4] it may be, but God will be in the voice, and the contrite spirit shall be revived.[5]

"What wilt thou that I should do unto thee?" A goodly word, indeed! What would not a soul, struggling in the depths and en-

[1] 1 Cor., i. 23. [2] Ps. lxxxv. 10. [3] Acts, iv. 11, 12.
[4] 1 Kings, xix. 12. [5] Is., lvii. 15.

tanglements of sin, give once to hear it from his Lord? Let us admire,

I. The fulness of the grace. The tender love of Christ to lost souls is a great deep, without bottom and without shore. The wing of no angel can bear him so high that he can look over all its extent. The guilt of no sinner has been able to sound all its depth. The countless multitudes, who have been washed in its waters, have not diminished its abundance nor impaired its virtue.

King Ahasuerus said unto Queen Esther at the banquet of wine, What is thy petition? and it shall be granted thee; and what is thy request? even to the half of my kingdom shall it be performed.[1] And so the monarchs of the East delighted to speak. But their utmost promise was *half* the kingdom, and their kingdoms were earthly, bounded and unsubstantial, and their pompous generosity often but the flourishing rhetoric of lust, pride and wine.

But Jesus puts no limit to His offers. Ask, it shall be given you. Ask, and ye shall receive, that your joy may be full. Whatsoever

[1] Esther, v. 6.

ye shall ask in my name, that will I do.[1] In Him are hid all the treasures of wisdom and knowledge.[2] All power is given unto Him in heaven and in earth.[3] He is the head of all power.[4] All things were created by Him and for Him.[5] In Him dwelleth all the fulness of the Godhead bodily.[6] His word can open heaven to the vilest sinner: yea, His smile can *make* a heaven in the saddest heart. A crust from Him is a feast, and the feast which He shall spread in heaven for His saints shall banquet the soul through Eternity. He is Heir of all things,[7] and, at the believing call of the meanest beggar, He will make that beggar a joint-heir with Him,[8] to an inheritance incorruptible, undefiled, and that fadeth not away[9]—an exceeding and eternal weight of glory.[10] When we are Christ's Christ is ours; and then all things are ours—apostles, Scriptures, dispensations, ordinances, life and death, this world and the next, things present and

[1] Mat., vii. 7; John, xvi. 24; xiv. 13. [2] Col., ii. 3.
[3] Mat., xxviii. 18. [4] Col., ii. 10. [5] Col., i. 16.
[6] Col., ii. 9. [7] Heb., i. 2. [8] Rom., viii. 17.
[9] 1 Pet., i. 4. [10] 2 Cor. iv. 17.

things to come; all are ours.[1] Well might the Apostle count all things loss for Christ.[2] Such loss is infinite gain. With the Lord Jesus Christ, afflictions are blessings, shame is honor, sickness is health, and death is life for evermore; out of weakness we are made strong,[3] in solitude we have the best company; our poverty turns to the true riches, our crosses to the sweetest comforts; nature gives way to grace, and grace issues in eternal glory.

II. Let us also admire the freeness of Christ's offers to lost sinners. The freeness of the offer springs from the fulness of the grace. "What wilt thou?" Choose for thyself, Bartimeus. If thou dost not carry away a noble gift, it is thine own fault. *I* do not set bounds to thy desires. The treasure is infinite, and thou hast it all to choose from.

The Spirit of the Lord is not straitened, and if we are, it is in ourselves.[3] The Lord's hand is not shortened, neither is His ear heavy; but our iniquities[4]—ah, there is the trouble! And no sin hides God's face sooner, or behind

[1] 1 Cor., iii. 21–23. [2] Phil., iii. 7. [3] Heb., xi. 34. Mic., ii. 7; 2 Cor., vi. 12. [4] Is., lix. 1, 2.

a darker cloud, than our unbelief. God's grace is always larger than man's desire, and freer than his faith.[1] We continually need His exhortation to Israel, Open thy mouth wide and I will fill it.[2] One prayer should be ever on our lips, Lord, increase our faith![3] If this day our fleece is dry, it is not because there is no dew in heaven, nor because none fell last night.[4] If we take little pitchers to the well, we shall carry little water away. Though the golden bowl be full of golden oil, the lamp will burn dim, if the golden pipe be narrow or choked.[5] The ocean itself can pour but a scanty stream through a slender channel. And when sinners cry, I have no grace, it is because unbelief has shut up their bosoms. Or when the people of God cry, My leanness! my leanness![6] it is because their narrow faith suffers them only to taste where they might drink—only to snatch crumbs with the dogs, while they might sit down with the children at the table, and feast on all the savory things with which Christ spreads His board.

[1] Eph., iii. 20. [2] Ps. lxxxi. 10. [3] Luke, xvii. 5.
[4] Judges, vi. 40. [5] Zech., iv. 2, 12. [6] Is., xxiv. 16.

'Whosoever' and 'whatsoever' are two precious words often in the mouth of Christ. Whosoever will may come.[1] Whatsoever ye shall ask in my name, that will I do.[2] 'Whosoever' is on the outside of the gate, and lets in all who choose. 'Whatsoever' is on the inside, and gives those who enter the free range of all the region and treasury of grace. 'Whosoever' makes salvation free, 'Whatsoever' makes it full.

III. See how Christ's grace condescends to every soul's peculiar need. He will suit His granting to our asking. To every soul He says, "What wilt *thou?*"

It is marvellous and beautiful to observe how various are the voices of free grace. "I am thirsty," says one. "Come to the waters," she cries.[3] "I am hungry," says another. "Then eat ye that which is good," she says, "and let your soul delight itself in fatness."[4] "But I am poor, and have nothing to buy with." "Come, buy wine and milk without money, and without price."[5] "We are weary,"

[1] Rev., xxii. 17; John, vii. 37. [2] John, xiv. 13.
[3] Is., lv. 1. [4] Is., lv. 2. [5] Is., lv. 1.

sigh the laborers in the sun-beaten fields. "Come unto me," breathes her answer like a breeze from the waters, "and I will give you rest."[1] "Cast thy burden on the Lord and He will sustain thee,"[2] she whispers to the pilgrim ready to faint on the highway. "Behold the Fountain," she cries to the guilty, "the Fountain opened for sin and uncleanness."[3] To the lost she cries, "I am the Way;" to the ignorant, "I am the Truth;" to the dying, "I am the Life."[4] How large her welcome to the sinner, how soothing her consolations to the mourner, how inspiring her tones to him that is faint of heart! There is no disease for which she has not a remedy, no want for which she has not a supply; and every one who applies to her shall confess at length, "It is enough; I am blessed as if all the methods and riches of grace were for me alone!"

IV. This question teaches that, though Christ knows what we want and what He will do, He will have us express our wants.

Prayer is not giving information to God;

[1] Mat., xi. 28.
[2] Ps. lv. 22.
[3] Zech., xiii. 1.
[4] John, xiv. 6.

that His Omniscience does not need:[1] nor does it change His will; that His Immutability cannot suffer.[2] It does not awaken His grace, for it is from everlasting; nor increase it, for it is infinite. But it opens a way for grace to flow according to its own eternal plan. It is faith's answer to Christ's question, "What wilt thou?" It lives only as grace quickens it, and speaks only as grace teaches it. There is no true prayer till God pours out His Holy Spirit —the Spirit of grace and supplications.[3] He is first the Spirit of grace, implanting holy affections, and then the Spirit of supplications, turning these affections into earnest desires, which breathe from the heart in prayer, even as the same Spirit helpeth our infirmities.[4]

Through all the cold, dark night the petals cf the flower were shut. So the sun found it, and poured his rays upon it, till its heart felt the warmth. Then it yearned to be filled with these pleasant beams, and opened its bosom to drink them in. And so it is with man's prayer and God's grace.

[1] Mat., vi. 8.
[2] James, i. 17.
[3] Zech., xii. 10.
[4] Rom., viii. 26.

"The blind man said unto Him, Lord, that I might receive my sight!" How prompt and to the point is this answer. Let sinners and saints learn from it to distinguish among their wants, and keep their greatest needs uppermost. Bartimeus lacked many things, and Christ's question has given him a wide range, but we hear only, "My sight! my sight!"

How pointless are the prayers we often hear. They scatter weakly over the whole ground. They have no aim and do no execution. It may be a time of declension or revival, a day of thanksgiving or fasting, it may be family worship or a Church-business meeting—it matters not; you shall hear pretty much the same prayer. And if you come back five years after, you shall find the good man still going over his old beat, as if the church and the world and he had made no progress, and suffered no change.

If we would pray well, we must have something to pray for—something we really crave. We must know our wants, feel our wants, express our wants. We must have "an errand at the Throne." I learned that expression from a pious old slave. He was asked the secret of the fervor and spirit with which he always prayed. "O," said he, "I always have an errand at the Throne, and then I just tell the Lord what I come for, and wait for an answer." Thus too shall we wait for an answer. Suppose Bartimeus, after kneeling in the dust, and raising his bitter cry, "Lord, that I might receive my sight," had then turned from Christ and said, "Well, I have prayed; now I will beg a little;" and so, rising from his knees, he goes begging through the whole crowd. Would he not deserve that the insulted Saviour should spurn his prayer, and seal his blindness to him for ever? But what else do *we*, when after the false fervors of our shallow prayers, we dry our eyes, and go wandering after every earthly gain and pleasure? when we do not watch for an answer and wait for its coming? Even the sportsman, who cares not for his game, follows the arrow with his eye, till he sees it strike. But how many never cast a second glance after a prayer which has left their lips!

But Bartimeus did not, could not, turn

away from Christ. If his lips do not still cry, "My sight! my sight!" a mightier prayer than lips can utter is going forth from his heart. You may see it in the whole attitude —the clasped hands, the out-stretched neck, the up-turned face in a very agony of longing, the panting breast, beaten inwardly by the tumultuous heart, the sightless balls "rolling in vain" to find the day, and straining toward Jesus, as if they would force a pathway for light!

Not long "in vain," O blind man, not long! The morning cometh. The Sun is about to rise upon thee with healing in His wings![1]

[1] Mal., iv. 2.

VIII.

"So Jesus had compassion, and touched his eyes, and said unto him, Receive thy sight: go thy way: thy faith hath saved thee."

"SO Jesus had compassion;" surely not then for the first time, but then it was more manifest—its proofs were given. There was fragrance in the alabaster box before it was broken by the violence of love, but then its ointment poured forth, and its precious odors filled the room.[1] Such holy violence there is in prayer, and so God's treasured blessings are obtained. Christ's secret pity begets our petitions, which then His open compassion accepts and crowns. Jesus loved Martha and her sister and Lazarus, when far away; but when He stood at the grave He wept.[2] And we may believe that, whenever the sad fruits of sin were thus before Him, His face gave

[1] Mark, xiv. 3. [2] John, xi. 5, 35.

token of His heart. Then the love which brought Him to die, that He might redeem, would stir more mightily within His soul, and overflow in looks and words and deeds of pity. It was at such a moment that Matthew was moved to make the record, "Jesus had compassion."

"And touched his eyes." This was not of necessity, as if His blessing could not flow without a medium, but in lowliness and kindness.

He could have healed with a word merely, or, if He had pleased, without a word, and far off as well as near. But He generally chose some outward instrumentality. He put clay on the eyes of the man blind from his birth, and sent him to wash in the pool of Siloam.[1] He had the stone taken from the sepulchre of Lazarus before He cried "Come forth!"[2] He multiplied the loaves and fishes already at hand, instead of astonishing the multitude by a pure creation.[3]

His lowly spirit is seen in this; for thus His miracles were shorn of some of the rays

[1] John, ix. 6, 7. [2] John, xi. 39. [3] John, vi. 11

most dazzling to sense. He remembered that though He was the Fellow of Jehovah,[1] He had now become His Servant, and He dealt prudently.[2] Though He was over all, God blessed for ever, He was now manifest in the flesh,[3] and, as became Him, He veiled His uncreated splendor, and modestly wrought His glorious works.

But while there was the hiding of His power[4] from the multitude, He the more revealed His kindness to His patients. When the leper found that Christ dreaded no pollution, even ceremonial, from his touch;[5] when the deaf man, who could not hear His words, *felt* His fingers in his ears;[6] when the poor woman, whom Satan had kept so cruelly bent for eighteen years, felt the hands of One mightier than the old Tyrant, laid lovingly upon her;[7] doubtless their very flesh thrilled at the touch, and their faith was made strong to believe all that He had promised.

Who does not envy Bartimeus that gentle

[1] Zech., xiii. 7. [2] Is., lii. 13. [3] Rom., ix. 5; 1 Tim., iii. 16.
[4] Hab., iii. 4. [5] Mark, i. 41. [6] Mark, vii. 33.
[7] Luke, xiii. 13, 16.

resting of the fingers of Jesus on his eyes? Rather let us strive to feel His blessed Spirit in our hearts, and we shall taste a sweetness which will leave no room for envy.

"And said, Receive thy sight." An echo from within the Veil! "Lord, that I might receive my sight!" cried the suppliant without. "Receive thy sight!" answers the Sovereign within. Weak and tremulous, with its burden of anguish, is the voice from the dust. Clear and joyous, with power and blessing, is the Voice from the Throne. I call that goodly music, O friends! The Eternal Spirit is its Author. He searcheth all things, even the deep things of God,[1] and finding there what the Father designs to give, He teaches us to desire and ask accordingly. His intercession within us is "according to God," says the Apostle; that is, "according to the will of God," rightly supply the translators.[2] And so, if Christ suits His granting to our asking, it is because the Spirit has first shaped our asking to His granting. The purpose of grace is the foundation of the prayer

[1] 1 Cor., ii. 10. [2] Rom., viii. 27.

of faith. Eternal Grace is the mould into which faith is cast. Therefore there is harmony between faith and grace. "Grace crowns what grace begins."

Oh, to hear more of that music! If all sinners and all saints would thus cry together to heaven, our earth would hear such voices ringing in the air above it, as if the heavenly host had again come down, harping and praising with the notes of "Peace," and "Glory," as of old above the plains of Bethlehem.[1]

"Go thy way." There is but one word in the Greek for these three. It is a mere formula of dismission in peace.

"Thy faith hath saved thee." In our English Bibles we read this expression in Luke, but in Mark, "Thy faith hath made thee whole." Both answer, however, to one phrase in the original, and should not differ in the translation. Yet there is little to choose between them. 'Save' is the exact rendering of the Greek word, but 'making whole' is one form of saving. There are many kinds and degrees of salvation, even as the evils vary

[1] Luke, ii. 13, 14.

from which we need deliverance. This man's malady was physical, and he was saved by the healing of his flesh. If this was all, the more general word, 'save,' would here take its special meaning, 'to make whole.' If, however, he was also, up to this moment, an unpardoned sinner, he needed a great spiritual deliverance and healing. And if this too was granted as his eyes were opened, then he was 'made whole' in the highest sense, saved wholly and for ever from the double curse under which he suffered.

However this may have been, it is enough for us that his salvation was by his faith. God has linked faith and salvation together by more than "hooks of steel," even by His unchangeable decree. No decrees of God are more certain than these; He that believeth shall he saved, and, He that believeth not shall be damned.[1] He that believeth *is* passed already from death to life,[2] while he that believeth not is condemned already.[3] The moment of faith is the moment of stepping from the region of the curse to the region of the

[1] Mark, xvi. 16. [2] John, v. 24. [3] John, iii. 18.

blessing. The region of unbelief is black with God's frown, and filled with plagues and wrath; but the region of faith is as the floor of heaven for brightness. Christ's righteousness shelters it, the graces of the Spirit beautify it, and the eternal smile of God comforts and glorifies it. These regions may be near together and touch like circles; and while a man is stepping from one to the other, he may feel both joy and anguish;—Lord I believe!—help Thou mine unbelief![1]

Unbelief is a devil. He was born in hell and reigns there. With one hand he ever keeps his hold on hell, while with the other he has seized the earth and wrenched it from its sphere, and he is always striving to drag it down into his own blackness and ruin. But the hand of faith takes hold of heaven. What wonder then, that our poor world ever trembles and wavers so, in the struggle of these mighty powers?

And thus it is that "faith saves." There was nothing in this blind man's soul that could open his eyes, but through grace there

[1] Mark, ix. 24.

was something in him that could take hold of Christ.

And so "faith saves" and grace saves;[1] faith as the instrument, and grace as the divine efficiency; faith the channel, and grace the heavenly stream; faith the finger that touches the garment's fringe, and grace the virtue that pours from the Saviour's heart.[2] Faith cannot scale the dreadful precipice from which nature has fallen, but it can lay hold on the rope which grace has let down even into its hands from the top, and which it will draw up again with all the burden faith can bind to it. And this is all the mystery of faith's saving. Christ reaches down from heaven, and faith reaches up from earth, and each hand grasps the other; one in weakness, the other in power. Yea, the hand of faith is often but a poor, benumbed hand, stretched out in anguish from the dark flood where the soul is sinking.

Neither faith nor grace saves alone; grace will not, faith cannot. Therefore is salvation by faith, and salvation by grace. Yet grace

[1] Eph., ii. 5. [2] Luke, viii. 44, 46.

has the highest place. When brought together, grace is the efficiency and faith the medium for its flow; saved, says Paul, *by* grace *through* faith.[1] And even faith is of grace. Salvation, (or the promise which contains it,) says Paul again, is of faith, that it might be of grace, and to the end, he argues, that it may be sure.[2] That all may be sure, all must be given. Whatever is of me is uncertain; whatever is of God cannot fail. Therefore my faith, which receives salvation, is not left to be my work; it is one of the fruits of the operation of God. Thus, while there *must* be faith, there *will* be, if there is grace. And so it turns out, after all, that salvation is *all* of grace. Blessed be God for that! Of myself I had no more power to believe than to love, or be holy, or clothe myself with righteousness and walk into heaven. For my carnal mind was *enmity* against God. It was not subject to the law of God, nor, indeed, could it be.[3] But God, who is rich in mercy, for His great love wherewith He loved us, even when we were dead in sins, hath quickened us together with Christ.[4]

[1] Eph., ii. 8. [2] Rom., iv. 16. [3] Rom., viii. 7. [4] Eph., ii. 4, 5.

IX.

"Immediately he received his sight."

IN these words we reach that point in this history where all its lines of interest meet—that wonderful moment when the power of Jesus wrought miraculously on the eyes of Bartimeus, and he was blind no more.

How much was crowded into that moment! The accomplished purpose of loving-kindness, and the answered prayer of misery; the true Light shining, and the darkness not failing, now, to comprehend it;[1] the Saviour's power and grace victorious, and the helpless sinner the subject of a change so immediate, so amazing and so blessed, that from this moment he rejoiced to be bound in the free captivity of Jesus; while so clear was the shining of Deity in all that was done, that not only was the Son of Man glorified thereby, but the beams

[1] John, i. 5.

shot far up and rested on the invisible Throne. For "Bartimeus followed Jesus in the way, glorifying God, and all the people, when they saw it, gave praise unto God."

Nor shall we, I trust, be able to refrain from 'glorifying' with Bartimeus, and 'praising' with the multitude; saying, Surely this is fruit worthy of the Tree of Life, on whose boughs it shall for ever hang, mirrored by the River of God and admired by all who sing of the work and death of Jesus.

Oh for a breath upon my soul from that eternal shore, that I may not utterly fail in speaking of this gracious mystery!

I. What, then, does this healing stand for in the higher, spiritual world?

Surely, nothing less than Regeneration—the new birth of the soul. Of the many images employed by the Holy Ghost, to set forth our natural state, perhaps none is more frequent than blindness. Darkness is ever the chosen symbol of the kingdom of Satan, and light of the Kingdom of God. Darkness, corruption and death are used interchangeably, and so are light, purity and life. Satan is the Prince of Darkness, his dwelling is under darkness,[1] his power is to blind all who follow him,[2] and they too are at last cast into outer darkness,[3] a land of darkness, as darkness itself, where even the light is as darkness.[4] But God is light, and in Him is no darkness at all.[5] He is the Father of lights. He dwelleth in the light which no man can approach unto.[6] His children are children of light.[7] They walk in the light, even as He is the light,[8] and are themselves light in the Lord.[9] Christ's mission, therefore, is often set forth as an opening of the eyes of the blind.[10] He came that they which see not, might see.[11]

Most naturally therefore is the new birth described as a transition from darkness to light, a translation from the kingdom of Satan to the Kingdom of God's dear Son.[12] Thus Paul sets the natural and gracious states of the Ephesians in vivid contrast; Ye were some time darkness, but now are ye light in

[1] Jude, 6. [2] 2 Cor., iv. 4. [3] Mat., xxii. 13.
[4] Job, x. 22. [5] 1 John, i. 5. [6] 1 Tim., vi. 16.
[7] 1 Thes., v. 5. [8] 1 John, i. 7. [9] Eph., v. 8.
[10] Is., xlii. 7. [11] John, ix. 39. [12] Col., i. 13.

the Lord.[1] Thus too, Christ connects the symbol with its reality, in sending Paul to the Gentiles, to open their eyes, and turn them from darkness to light, and from the power of Satan unto God.[2]

The suitableness of these symbols needs no vindication. Every heart feels their fitness. They have gone into all languages and all mythologies. I have forgotten whose thought it is, that no man ever set forth purity or blessedness, truth, glory or God, under the image of darkness, nor could light ever have seemed the fit image of evil or death.

By Christ's constant miracles of healing the blind, and by the constant use of them in setting forth the mystery of regeneration, the Holy Ghost teaches us three important lessons.

1. That the new birth is from God. If the harp be broken, the hand of the maker may repair it, and wake the chords again to their old power and sweetness. There is hope of a tree, if it be cut down, that it will sprout again, and that the tender branch thereof will not cease. Though the root thereof wax old

[1] Eph., v. 8. [2] Acts, xxvi. 18.

in the earth, and the stock thereof die in the ground, yet through the scent of water it will bud and bring forth boughs like a plant.[1]

But who can restore the shattered crystal, so that the sunbeams shall stream through it without finding a flaw, and flash, once more, as of old, in the ever-changing play of their splendor?

And who can open the eyes of the blind? Who can restore to that most lustrous and precious of gems, its expression and power, when distorted and blotted by disease or violence? Who shall open again those delicate pathways for the light of two worlds—the outer world shining in and filling the soul with images of beauty, and that inner world shining out in joy, love and thankfulness? Surely none but the Maker of this curious frame, who, when sin had so cruelly marred it, came in compassion as infinite as His might, to be Redeemer and Restorer where He had already been Creator. Only He can open the eyes of the blind. The power of God is in that work.

But if a man *die* shall he live again?[2] Oh,

[1] Job, xiv. 7–9.

[2] Job, xiv. 14.

if the *soul* be dead, dead in guilt and corruption and the curse of Almighty God, can it revive? Yes, thanks be to God, by reason of the working of His mighty power, which He wrought in Christ, when He raised Him from the dead,[1] (after He had been delivered for our offences,[2]) we, also, may be quickened, who were dead in trespasses and sins, and children of wrath, we may be quickened together with Christ; for we are His workmanship, created in Christ Jesus unto good works.[3]

Then let men beware how they disparage God's glory in the regeneration of human souls. If it was blasphemy without forgiveness to ascribe the miracles of Jesus to the working of Satan,[4] *their* sin is not easily measured, who ascribe this higher work on man's ruined soul, of which those bodily cures were but types, to any power but that of God. Not by eloquence, not by ordinances, not by the soul's own resolution, not by God's holy truth itself, without the added and immediate power

1 Eph., i. 19, 20.
2 Rom., iv. 25.
3 Eph., ii. 1, 3, 5, 10.
4 Mark, iii. 22–30.

of the Holy Ghost, is the soul born again. To Him then be the undivided glory!

2. In the light of this miracle we also learn that, whatever activities the sinner may put forth before and after his regeneration, *in* the great change he is passive. Under the moving of the Spirit, he may, like Bartimeus, cry for the blessing before it comes; like him he may rejoice when it does come, and be ever after constrained to a grateful holiness; but in effecting the change, like Bartimeus, he does, simply, nothing.

All the agonies of the blind man, all his tears and cries, all his rolling and straining his sightless balls, had just nothing at all to do with the act of restoration. That was Christ's alone. Only His activity availed or even entered there. The blind man was the passive recipient of the miraculous power.

And so in the new birth;—"born of God,"[1] tells it all. It is the "unparticipated work"[2] of the Holy Ghost.

In this, regeneration is distinguished from conversion. God turns the man, but the man,

[1] John, i. 13. [2] Professor Butler.

so moved, turns with his whole heart. It is the day of God's great "power," but also of the sinner's great "willingness."[1] "Conversion," says Fisher, in his Catechism, "is the spiritual motion of the whole man toward God in Christ, as the immediate effect of the real and supernatural change that is wrought in regeneration." The fire which the sun has kindled mounts toward it at once. The kindling of the heavenly flame is regeneration; its upward motion, conversion. Regeneration is the divine cause, conversion the sure effect. Where there is the grace of life, there will be a life of grace.

3. Light did not open Bartimeus's eyes, nor does truth alone regenerate the sinner. Pouring light on blind eyes will not heal them. Flashing truth, even God's glorious truth, on the sinner's mind will not regenerate him. Bartimeus was as blind at noon as at midnight. The sinner is as blind under the blaze of the gospel, as amid the glooms of heathenism. The sinner hates the light. It is not a question of less or more with him, he hates

[1] Psalm cx. 3.

the very element. He hates God, and God is light. Truth is but the image of God, and is hated where He is hated. The carnal mind is enmity against God, say the Scriptures.[1] Then follows by necessity the declaration, that it is not subject to the law of God, neither indeed can be. How strong the statements! How dreadful their connection! Absolute enmity against God, and necessary insubordination to His truth! Therefore before God or His holy law can be loved, the carnality of the soul must be destroyed, and that is the work of the Holy Ghost alone. Whatever part the truth may play, it cannot create. Only God does that.

II. Let me now speak of the greatness and glory of this change. I again speak simply of the bodily change wrought by the miracle in Bartimeus.

The bursting forth again of the sun from the clouds after many days of storm is as nothing to it, though a hundred landscapes are flooded with the splendor, and birds break out in song, and innumerable hearts leap up

[1] Rom., viii. 7.

to hail the clear heavens. Our thoughts rather go back to the day when God said, Let there be light,[1] and at once disclosed, to the gaze of the jubilant angels, a new world glowing with His unshadowed smile. This is the truer comparison. For here, too, in the breast of this suffering beggar, was a world of sensation and consciousness, a world even in its night and ruin nobler than earth or sun; for what is matter, in quantities however vast, and forms however excellent, to an immortal soul? Darkness has, indeed, long wrapped it, and wisdom been "from one entrance quite shut out." But now the same mighty word has spoken, and this living world is suddenly lighted through all its wondering, grateful depths. Think ye the angels had no song for this also?

Then who shall dare speak lightly of that work, in which God, who commanded the light to shine out of darkness, hath shined in our hearts, to give us the light of the knowledge of the glory of God in the face of Jesus Christ?[2] Are we not using language most

[1] Gen., i. 3. [2] 2 Cor., iv. 6.

accurately, when we call the new birth The Great Change? Is it not an event to be looked upon with astonishment? ever to be spoken of with reverence? Is it not a thing for everlasting amazement, that a guilty wretch, dead under the curse of God, should receive a communication of the divine life, be made a partaker of the divine nature,[1] and be adopted into the divine family? that he should be lifted from the dust of death to sit with princes on the heavenly hill? that from the pollutions of a hellish slavery, he should be exalted to the liberties and dignities, to the sanctity and blessedness of sonship with the Most High? Yea, that he should be a joint-heir with Christ,[2] and sit with Him in His Throne,[3] and reign with Him, in indissoluble union with Him, and participation with Him evermore in the honors and offices of His everlasting kingdom and priesthood?[4] Oh, if there were but *one* instance of this, would it not be for the glory of God and the wonder of heaven for ever? And shall it be less, when we have

[1] 2 Pet., i. 4. [2] Rom., viii. 17.
[3] Rev., iii. 21. [4] Rev., i. 6; v. 10.

but to lift up our eyes, and lo, a great multitude which no man can number, of all nations, and kindreds, and people, and tongues, standing before the throne, and before the Lamb?[1]

Well may the Apostle of love cry out with an admiration which even he cannot all express, Behold what manner of love the Father hath bestowed upon us, that we should be called the sons of God! And as his soul kindles along the line of our coming glory, exclaim again, confessing too how it passeth understanding, Beloved, now are we the sons of God, and it doth not yet appear what we shall be; but we know that when He shall appear, we shall be like Him, for we shall see Him as He is![2]

Well may the saints, for ever beholding, in the Lamb that was slain, the ground of their acceptance and the image of their sonship, sing in song for ever new, Unto Him that hath loved us, and washed us from our sins in His own blood, and hath made us kings and priests unto God and His Father, to Him be glory and dominion for ever and ever![3]

[1] Rev., vii. 9. [2] 1 John, iii. 1, 2. [3] Rev., i. 5, 6.

And shall we not bless, with equal praise, the good Spirit of our God, of whom we were born again,[1] in whose leading we have proof of our sonship,[2] and by whose effectual working we shall be changed into the very image of the glory for which we sigh?[3]—oh, *shall* we not bless Him, who is at once the Spirit of grace,[4] of life,[5] of adoption,[6] of help,[7] of prayer,[7] of liberty,[8] of comfort,[9] of sanctification,[10] of access,[11] of glory and of God?[12] Can we praise with a too boundless admiration that work on which the energies of the whole Godhead are expended, and by which the Perfections of Father, Son and Holy Ghost are chiefly seen for ever? Neander does not speak too strongly when he calls "the communication of the life of God to men," "the greatest of all miracles, the essence and aim of all, the standing miracle of all ages."

III. As "Bartimeus immediately received his sight," so in regeneration, the great change

[1] John, iii. 5. [2] Rom., viii. 14. [3] 2 Cor., iii. 18.
[4] Zech., xii. 10. [5] Rom., viii. 2. [6] Rom., viii. 15.
[7] Rom., viii. 26. [8] 2 Cor., iii. 17. [9] John, xiv. 16, 17.
[10] 1 Cor., vi. 11. [11] Eph., ii. 18. [12] 1 Pet., iv. 14..

is instantaneous. There is some one moment when the vision of the blind man, and the new life of the sinner begins. It may be feeble, but it has begun, and for the faintest beginning the creative act is needed. The case of that other blind man, who, at first, saw men as trees walking,[1] is not an illustration of gradual regeneration. Whenever it could be said that he saw, no matter how dimly, the great change was implied. However confused and weak his vision, it was real. . Before he was blind; now he sees. His whole state is changed, and is to be described by directly opposite expressions. Then he saw nothing, he could not see; now he can and does see. No farther change in the degree of his power to see can equal this, that from utter blindness, he should see at all.

And so in spiritual things; the kingdoms of darkness and light have no neutral frontier where their dominions mingle.[2] They are in deadliest opposition and sharpest contrast. One cannot be the subject of Christ and of Satan at the same time, nor in neutrality, sub-

[1] Mark, viii. 24.

[2] Mat., vi. 24.

ject to neither. He must be under either wrath or grace, either dead or alive. None can be both dead and alive; none can be neither dead nor alive.

But lest any draw a mistaken and discouraging inference, the case of that other blind man[1] is to be carefully regarded. Men may come slowly to their evidences of regeneration. Mists and darkness may still wrap the new creation. The sinner often frames for himself an ideal of conversion which leads to disappointment. His own imagination and the glowing accounts he has sometimes heard, cast a golden flush over his expected experience. But the Spirit sometimes grants only an experience of such a plain and commonplace character, that for a long time it never occurs to the sinner that *this* is the work for which he has waited in such high anticipation. In many cases, especially where grace reigns in early life, the Spirit's work, in its various stages from conviction to conscious enjoyment of pardoning love, is quiet, gradual, and almost imperceptible. At other times the Sov-

[1] Mark, viii. 22–26.

ereign Spirit may direct the sinner's eyes, at the moment of his illumination, chiefly to the guilt of his past life, or downward into the abysses of his own heart, or to the terrible majesty and exactions of God's holy law, and so fill him with renewed anguish. Comfort is not always the immediate result of the new birth. The sound of weeping may be the first that is heard.

Sometimes, too, the gloom disperses very slowly, and many a blacker cloud sweeps through it, till the soul is ready to despair. But in none of these cases is the soul left without sufficient attainable evidence that it is born of God.

Many are the souls who must say with holy Joseph Fletcher of Stepney, "it has often been the cause of much distress that I could not particularize the place, the time, the means of my conversion."

To know these things would indeed be pleasant, but let none be too anxious about them. Let them give all diligence to make their calling and election sure,[1] but be also

[1] 2 Peter, i. 10.

careful not to waste time and comfort in these fruitless inquiries, and embarrass the great question by that which does not concern it. The main thing for every sinner is, to be able on good ground, to say, Whereas I was blind, now I see.[1] If he can say this, and have the witness of the Spirit to its truth,[2] it matters little whether he is able to add, On such a day, in such a place, by such and such means, my eyes were opened.

A good ship has been broken by the tempest. Mast and rudder and compass, all are gone. The storm is over, but the wreck is drifting away blindly through night and fog. At length all is still, and the wondering sailors wait for the day. Tardily and uncertainly it dawns, and as the heavy mists slowly dissolve, all eyes are busy trying to discover where they are. At length one descries a cliff which seems familiar, another a pier in which he can hardly be mistaken, a third the old church spire, under whose shadow his mother is sleeping, and now, as the sun breaks forth, they all cry out in joyful assurance that they are in the

[1] John, ix. 25. [2] Rom., viii. 16.

desired haven! Mysteriously and without their aid, the Ruler of wind and wave has brought them there, and all are exulting in the great deliverance.

Nay, shall we say not all? Can you imagine one poor melancholy man refusing to rejoice, and even doubting these evidences, because he cannot tell the hour and angle of his arrival, nor whether he was borne chiefly by currents of air or ocean?

IV. On the blessedness of this change in Bartimeus—image of the spiritual blessedness of him who is first tasting that the Lord is gracious[1]—I can hardly bring myself to comment. The words of the evangelist, "immediately he received his sight," are the calm record of rapture beyond conception. Well does Addison call our sight the most perfect and most delightful of all our senses.[2] Well does Solomon exclaim, The light of the eyes rejoiceth the heart,[3] and cry out again, like one on whom a morning without clouds was dawning,[4] Truly the light is sweet, and a

[1] 1 Pet., ii. 3. [2] Spectator, No. 411.
[3] Prov., xv. 30. [4] 2 Sam., xxiii. 4.

pleasant thing it is for the eyes to behold the sun![1] Is it not beautiful that the eyes of a babe are scarcely opened on this world, before they follow the light and gaze on it as an absorbing wonder? After its needful nurture, its first joy is light—soft nurture, too, and stimulus, is it not?—for its little new-born soul. And why is it that *we* gaze unconsciously, but inevitably, on the ray that steals to us through chink or crevice, as we sit in reverie in a darkened room? Turn away as often and as resolutely as we will, if we forget again, the strong instinct of nature prevails, and our eyes fasten again upon the light. And who has not felt his soul blissfully swimming on the glories which pour, in amber and gold and crimson, from the setting sun? Though we have seen it a thousand times, we seek it again, and gaze, with adoring thankfulness, on the boundless canvas of transparent ether, on which the hand of God is spreading the colors of heaven. Our sense of joy is fresher, if not deeper, when even for a night the sight has been shadowed, and the

[1] Eccl., xi. 7.

eyes open on the advancing splendors of morning. And when after long imprisonment in the chamber of suffering, we go forth again, leaning, perhaps, on the arm of a congenial friend, to breathe once more the fresh air, and rejoice in the measureless freedom of nature, she seems to have clothed her green fields and forests, her blue skies and waters, in a brighter pomp of "summer bravery" than ever before, and the strange beauty fills and almost oppresses the soul. In what affecting terms does Dr. Kane describe the almost adoring rapture with which the return of the first sunshine was hailed, after the long horror of an Arctic night—the frozen blackness of months' duration, when he eagerly climbed the icy hills "to get the luxury of basking in its brightness," and made the grateful record, "To-day, blessed be the Great Author of light! I have once more looked upon the sun;" while his poor men, sick, mutilated, broken-hearted, and ready to die, crawled painfully from their dark berths to look upon his healing beams; when "every thing seemed superlative lustre and unsurpassable glory," when they could not refrain; they "oversaw the light."[1]

But what was this, what were all these, to the wonder and joy of Bartimeus's first vision of the mighty works of God? They already had the sense of sight, and had enjoyed many pleasureable exercises of it. To him the very sense was new, unimagined before. And now, at the word of Christ, the glorious element comes streaming, suddenly and for the first time, and in its fulness, with thrills of inconceivable bliss, upon the sense and soul buried from birth in utter darkness. Surely, on that day the light of the moon was as the light of the sun, and the light of the sun as the light of seven days.[2]

And what did he see first? Jesus, his best friend, his Saviour! Jesus, chiefest of ten thousand and altogether lovely;[3] O enviable lot! The first image which the light of heaven formed in his soul was the image of that dear face; O rich recompense for the long pains of blindness! The first employment of his eyes

[1] Arctic Expedition. Vol. II. [2] Is., xxx. 26.
[3] Song, v. 10.

was in beholding Him that opened them; O blessed consecration of his new powers and pleasures! He is still on his knees, fixed by the blessed vision where he had lately sunk in anguish and darkness. The eyes of Jesus are looking kindly down into *his* eyes, dilated and radiant with ecstacy. Gaze on, old man! Thou canst not look too ardently or too long. Never can thine eyes have nobler or purer joy on earth. Well mayst thou forget even sun and moon while He is before thee. In heaven itself all eyes are turned to Him. In heaven they need no sun nor moon, for He, the Brightness of the Father's glory, is the light thereof.[1]

But is the joy which attends spiritual illumination answerable to this? Not always (we have seen) as the immediate result. But it is attainable, and very soon the believer ought to have it, and, unless through ignorance, error, or guilt, will have it and that abundantly.

That this is so, the Scriptures every where prove, by their commands which make joy in

[1] Rev., xxi. 23; Heb., i. 3.

the Lord a duty;[1] by their frequent and most hearty exhortations, especially in the Psalms, —that book of religious experience; by their abounding declarations as to the blessedness of the righteous;[3] and by their exceeding great and precious promises,[4] full of the very cordial of heaven.[5]

Moreover the Bible is the sole Revealer of a conception of joy, in comparison with which every other idea of it, wherever found, is poor, earthly, and already darkened with the taint of death. It is a conception in which every best element of every earthly delight, by whatever name known—all the serenity of peace, all the exhilaration of hope, all the satisfaction of fruition, all the liveliness and sparkle of joy, all the mellower radiance of gladness, all the flush and bound of exultation, all the thrill and movement of rapture, are wrought into one surpassing combination, which chastened by holiness, softened by charity, dignified by immortality and transfused by the

[1] Phil., iv. 4. [2] Ps. xxxiii. 1. [3] Ps. i.; Mat., v. 3–12.
[4] 2 Pet., i. 4. [5] Ps. ciii. Many pages of references would not exhaust the Scriptures embraced under these heads.

beams of the all-encircling glory of the Godhead, is Blessedness.

It elevates the soul to know of such a state as possible for itself; it purifies it to hope for it; strengthens it to strive after it. What then must it be to taste it, as we may on earth, and drink it to the full, as we shall for ever in heaven!

Blessedness begins when the divine life has consciously begun, and progresses just as it is vigorous and unobstructed. For pleasure *must* spring from the flow of healthy life. If the life is from God, the pleasure must be godlike. As God is the Living One and the Blessed One, just as we participate in His life, we must also share His blessedness.

The soul is supremely blessed when it rests perfectly in God. That rest begins when He is seen by faith reconciled in Jesus Christ. It is consummated when faith is lost in sight. It begins on earth. It is perfected in heaven. But let it not be thought that either here or there it is a sluggish or even passive rest. It is inevitably active from the unceasing stir of energies for ever stimulated, for ever unexhausted. Yet indeed, there is a blessed passiveness too. Ever desiring, it is ever satisfied; and so, looking and loving, enlarging and filling, blessed and blessing, it goes on for ever.

This is the Bible idea of happiness. It is the perennial flow of the fountain into which the currents of the Infinite Ocean are pouring; the eternal going forth to God in love, or the life which He hath implanted in grace, and which He ever nourishes by perpetual communion in glory.

It has two elements, no more. It receives, it gives. If it cannot give, or will not, receiving is in vain. The active is a higher element than the passive. It is *more* blessed, says Christ, to give than to receive.[1] Yet is the passive first in necessity and order. Were there no receiving, there could be no giving.

Finally, if the new relations of a spiritually enlightened and renewed soul be considered, we cannot doubt the reality and greatness of its blessedness, both in the life which now is, and that which is to come.[2] The believer has been freed from the curse of the broken law, the wrath of God, the bondage of Satan and

[1] Acts, xx. 35. [2] 1 Tim., iv. 8.

the doom of hell. God has, in free grace, pardoned all his sins and accepted him as righteous in His sight, for the righteousness of Christ imputed to him. He has been received into the number, and has a right to all the privileges of the sons of God. He is renewed in the whole man after the image of God, and enabled more and more to die unto sin, and live unto righteousness. He may in this life partake in the unspeakable benefits of assurance of God's love, peace of conscience, joy in the Holy Ghost, increase of grace and perseverance therein to the end. He knows that his soul shall at death be made perfect in holiness, and immediately pass into glory; while his body, being still united to Christ, shall rest in its grave till the resurrection; and that then, being raised up in glory, he shall be openly acknowledged and acquitted in the day of judgment, and made perfectly blessed in the full enjoying of God to all eternity.

With these words, sublime as they are well known, I conclude what I had to say of the blessedness of the new birth.

X.

" And followed Jesus in the way."

THOUGH Jesus stood still at the beggar's call, He may stay no longer. This work is finished, and His mightier work on Calvary urges Him on.

But what shall Bartimeus do? Must they part so soon? Are his eyes no more to see His Lord? Have they been opened that he may know his gracious Friend, and taste the brief bliss of one moment's gaze, and then bid Him farewell? He would still see indeed, but the day would lack the warmth and glory it had before. Aye, his Sun would be set, and all that remained would be but as the stars gleaming coldly on the darkened earth. It cannot be. As Jesus turns to depart, he springs from the dust, and follows Him in the way.

Draw me, cries the Bride in the Song, as

soon as she catches sight of the royal chariot which bears her approaching Lord, Draw me, and we will run after Thee.[1] One glimpse of His beauty ravishes her soul with holy admiration. She would fly to His presence, and there she would abide. If He stands, like Mary, she would sit at His feet. If He removes, she would run after Him.

This simple phrase, "following Jesus," is comprehensive of the whole Christian life, and the many examples in the New Testament of following Him bodily are given, that we may understand what it is to follow Him spiritually. Christ has left us an example, says Peter, that we should follow His steps.[2] Archbishop Leighton, commenting on this passage, well reminds us that the word 'example' is 'copy' in the original—such a copy as children write after; whereof, he adds, "every step of His is a letter." Oh that the Holy Spirit may teach us to dip our pens in His dying love, and write after the blessed lines with a skilful hand!

Whoever has looked unto Jesus as the

[1] Song, i. 4. [2] 1 Peter, ii. 21.

Author of his faith, will look unto Him as the Finisher.[1] If the eyes be opened truly to see Him, the heart will be opened truly to love Him; and when the heart is thus enlarged, like David, we will run in the way of His commandments.[2] This is the test of discipleship; If any man serve Me, let him follow Me.[3] It is a mark found in all the saints; My sheep hear My voice, and I know them, and they follow Me.[4] The Psalmist speaks not for himself alone, but for all sound believers, when he cries, My soul followeth hard after Thee.[5] It was the salvation of Caleb and Joshua in the day of wrath, and is recorded as their glory for ever, that they wholly followed the Lord their God.[6] They found it, as all true pilgrims shall, the only path of safety, and the only one that, coming out of Egypt, stops not short of Canaan. To follow Jesus is the antidote of all error, doubt and despondency; it ensures our soundness in doctrine, our growth in grace, and our comforting, perpetual, and life-giving illumi-

[1] Heb., xii. 2. [2] Ps. cxix. 32. [3] John, xii. 26. [4] John, x. 27. [5] Psalm lxiii. 8. [6] Num., xxxii. 11, 12; Josh., xiv. 6–14.

nation. All this is in the words of Christ; I am the Light of the world: He that followeth Me shall not walk in darkness, but shall have the light of life.[1] And here, too, we find the high, eternal service and blessedness of the saints. It is the glory and joy of the one hundred and forty and four thousand, redeemed from the earth as the first fruits unto God and the Lamb, that they follow the Lamb whithersoever He goeth.[2]

O friends, let *us* follow Him whithersoever He goeth. Let us follow Him "in the way"—the way laid down in His Word, the way opened by His Providence, the way of which the Spirit whispers, This is the way, walk ye in it.[3] It may lead thee into great and sore troubles; but when thou passest through the waters, He will be with thee, and through the rivers, they shall not overflow thee; when thou walkest through the fire, thou shalt not be burned; neither shall the flame kindle upon thee.[4] It may be a way of which we cannot see the end, nay, in which we must walk

[1] John, viii. 12.
[2] Rev., xiv. 4.
[3] Is., xxx. 21.
[4] Is., xliii. 2.

softly,[1] groping and wondering. Let us be of good heart, and still hope in God; for we shall yet praise Him for the help of His countenance. At evening-time, it shall be light.[2]

Sometimes His way is in the sea, and His path in the great waters, and His footsteps are not known. Then the voice of His thunder is in the heavens, the waters are afraid, the depths also are troubled. But it is only His enemies who need be in fear and dread. These tremendous preparations may, indeed, intimidate even His own people for a while, and they may tremble as they find that *His* awful pathway must be theirs. But soon even the women of Israel are exulting, with timbrel and dance, on the shore of liberty, in the glorious triumphing of their God.[3]

The path of many of us may lie much in the Valley of Humiliation—a life of obscurity, poverty and lowly toil. We may be Christ's hidden ones [4] all our days. Or, we may be brought down to dwell here, after having walked in high places. Now, the descent to

[1] Is., xxxviii. 15. [2] Ps. xlii. 5; Zech., xiv. 7.
[3] Ps. lxxvii. 16–20; Ex., xv. 20, 21. [4] Ps. lxxxiii. 3.

this valley, says Bunyan, is "steep," and "the way slippery;" and who hath not found it so? Yet it was among its green meadows "beautiful with lilies," that Mr. Great-heart and the pilgrims heard the cheerful song of the Shepherd's boy, who wore so much of "the herb called heart's-ease in his bosom." And here "our Lord formerly had His country-house; He loved much to be here; He loved also to walk in these meadows, and He found the air was pleasant."

Yes, humble pilgrims! be sure ye shall find your Lord's foot-prints set thickly here. There you may see the stable in which He was born,[1] the humble home in which He lived,[2] the shop in which He toiled,[3] the mountain-side where He prayed through all the long night.[4] See the paths going all over the valley, all worn by His feet, and stopping so often at the abodes of the suffering and poor.[5] There He sat and wept over the guilty and lost,[6] and there He took the little babes and blessed

[1] Luke, ii. 7.
[2] Luke, ii. 39, 51.
[3] Mark, vi. 3.
[4] Luke, vi. 12.
[5] Mat., iv. 23; xi. 5.
[6] Luke, xix. 41

them.[1] See, too, the place of His anguish, of His trial, of His bloody death![2] And there is His tomb, but with the stone rolled away, and empty now![3] And there is the upper chamber, where He breathed that peace which still hovers over this valley like an air of balm.[4] And there He lifted up His hands and ascended to His Father and your Father, His God and your God.[5]

So thy way, believer, must lie by the Cross and the grave. But beyond the grave is the resurrection, and then the crown of life for ever. Fear not then to follow the Good Shepherd. Let the Twenty-third Psalm teach thee, in a gracious summary, how and where He will lead thee, and what He will do for thee by the way; and I think thou wilt be ready to say with Mr. Standfast, as he stood in the River of death, "Wherever I have seen the print of His shoe in the earth, there I have coveted to set my foot too." Look, then, evermore to Jesus, thy Precursor, and therefore Exemplar

[1] Mark, x. 13–16. [2] Mat., xxvi. 36, 57; xxvii. 2, 33.
[3] Mat., xxviii. 2, 6. [4] John, xx. 19.
[5] John, xx. 17; Luke, xxiv. 50.

in all the way of faith and obedience,[1] and cry unto Him, even as He cried, in the days of His flesh,[2] to His Father, Thou wilt show me the path of life! In Thy presence is fulness of joy; at Thy right hand are pleasures for evermore![3]

[1] Heb., xii. 2, 3. [2] Heb., v. 7. [3] Psalm xvi. 11

XI.

"Glorifying God."

WHEN his eyes found their noblest joy, his tongue was put to its noblest use. It is the glory of the tongue that it can glorify God.[1] Filled with irrepressible gladness, he broke forth in loud thanksgivings and praises. He began to sing in the ways of the Lord[2] as soon as he entered them. He had reached the fourth and brightest link of that gracious succession revealed in Psalm l. 15; trouble leading to prayer, prayer issuing in deliverance, and deliverance in glorifying. As he looked around on the goodly frame of nature, and felt the streams of God's gracious benignity flowing into his consciousness, he was constrained to

> "bear some humble part
> In that immortal song,"

which is sung in that world, in which both

[1] James, iii. 9. [2] Psalm cxxxviii. 5.

creation and redemption are glorified; Great and marvellous are Thy Works, Lord God Almighty! Just and true are Thy Ways, Thou King of saints! Who shall not fear Thee, O Lord, and glorify Thy name?[1]

Whoso offereth praise glorifieth Me, says God.[2] There were three ways in which Bartimeus glorified Him, and none can glorify Him in any other way;—in thought, word and deed; by his heart's secret gladness and adoration, by his audible and public praise, and by his following Jesus in the way. The first was the fruit of the soul, the second the fruit of the lips, the third the fruit of the life. The first was visible to God alone, the second and third were manifest to men. The first was the hidden spring of both the others; for the thanksgiving of the soul is the soul of thanksgiving, and where it is wanting, the professions of the mouth and the works of the life are dead and offensive;—the loathsome offering of hypocrisy. But if the lips and life have not their offerings also, the praise of the soul is without its needful outlets and

[1] Rev., xv. 3, 4. [2] Psalm l. 23.

evidences, and like faith without works, is dead, being alone.[1] If through sloth or cowardice in speaking and acting for God, a bushel is put over the light,[2] it will not only be concealed but smothered. The true light, the light of God's kindling, will, indeed, according to the proverb, burn through the bushel.[3] If there is abundance in the heart, the mouth *will* speak.[4] Art thou still dumb? Then thy heart's fancied abundance is emptiness. Religion not in the soul is mockery. Religion in the soul only is impossibility. We must first *be* light, ourselves lighted from the Sun of Righteousness, and then our light must shine before men, that they may see our good works. So only can we lead others to glorify our Father who is in heaven, and thereby ourselves most effectually glorify Him.[5]

Dr. Doddridge once exerted himself to procure the pardon of a man condemned to die. When he succeeded and hastened to the cell with the glad news, and the prison door was flung open, the poor man cast himself to the

[1] James, ii. 17.
[2] Mat., v. 15.
[3] Stier. Words of the Lord Jesus.
[4] Mat., xii. 34.
[5] Mat., v. 14–16.

earth, and clasping the feet of his deliverer, exclaimed, "Every drop of my blood thanks you, for you have saved them all!"

Such full-voiced expression of the heart's gratitude was heard from the men also whom Christ delivered from their plagues. The dumb began to sing, the lame to leap, and all to testify, in some open, lively way, how thankful they were for such mercies. Only once do we hear that mournful question and complaint, Were there not ten cleansed? but where are the nine? There are not found that returned to give glory to God, save this stranger![1]

The piety of the primitive church was of the same cheerful, out-spoken type. And when we go back to the more ancient ages, and climb the hill of Zion, what bursts of jubilant music greet us! What ringing of harps, what pealing of organs, with the voice of psalms, like the swell of the sea! Hearken: Come and hear, all ye that fear God, and I will declare what He hath done for my soul.[2] I will bless the Lord at all times; His praise

[1] Luke, xvii. 17, 18. [2] Psalm lxvi. 16.

shall continually be in my mouth. O magnify the Lord with me, and let us exalt His name together![1] O sing unto the Lord a new song! Sing unto the Lord! Bless His name![2] For it is a good thing to give thanks unto the Lord, and to sing praises unto Thy name, O most High! for it is pleasant, and praise is comely.[3] Let the children of Zion be joyful in their King![4]

Alas, how many who profess to be Zion's children in our day, seem even ashamed of their King! They have no glad story to tell of His dealings with their souls, no harp to sweep in His praise, no apostrophes to heaven and earth, to field and flood and the saints of God, challenging them to mingle their voices in celebrating redeeming grace.

But why do I speak of harps and apostrophes? There are men and women who profess to have been healed by the Lord Jesus of their soul's deadly malady, and yet can hardly bring themselves to speak a word in His praise in any company. Is He evil-spoken of?

[1] Ps. xxxiv. 1, 3.
[2] Ps. xcvi. 1, 2.
[3] Ps. xcii. 1; cxlvii. 1.
[4] Ps. cxlix. 2.

They will not defend Him. Is He well-spoken of? They have no word to add. Is He not spoken of at all? He never will be, if they must begin. The beauty, excellency and glory of His person, offices and work; all His condescension, grace and tenderness; all the events of His life, all the sufferings of His death; all His exaltation, reign and second coming, seem not to be enough to loosen their tongues, or give them anything at all to say.

Nay, more: they see their blind neighbors groping their way down to endless night, but cannot go to them and recommend the Heavenly Physician. If an earthly physician is needed, they are at once voluble and bold. They can tell you how kind he is, what cures he has wrought, and where he is to be found. But let the soul be in danger, and they are dumb.

Shall I go further? Yes, there are fathers and mothers, who are ashamed to tell the story of their healing to their own poor, blind sons and daughters, who have inherited from them the dreadful woe. They pity them;

they know they will perish if they come not to Christ; they will be glad if "the minister" will speak to them; but *they* cannot. They are ashamed to be heard by their own families speaking *to* Jesus. Even in the sanctuary of home they dare not call their offspring about them, and kneeling before His feet, bless Him, in simplest words, for His mercy, and then cry, "Lord, look now upon these poor blind children, and heal them!"

Can we wonder that God withholds the joy of His salvation[1] from such base cowardice? Oh, let us wonder that He withholds His wrath! Blessed Jesus, if Thou didst die for me, shall I not live for Thee? If Thou didst suffer for me, shall I not speak for Thee? If Thou wast not ashamed of my shame, shall I be ashamed of thy glory? If my sins once laid on Thee, made Thee dumb, like a sheep before her shearers,[2] shall not Thy graces wrought in me, open my lips that my mouth may show forth Thy praise, and my tongue sing aloud of Thy righteousness? [3]

[1] Ps. li. 12. [2] Is., liii. 6, 7. [3] Ps. li. 14, 15.

XII.

"And all the people, when they saw it, gave praise unto God."

A SINGLE beam of light becomes a star on the bosom of a thousand drops of the morning. The song of one is followed by the chorus of many. The rejoicing of Bartimeus has made the highway to Jerusalem like the garden of the Lord; joy and gladness are found therein, thanksgiving and the voice of melody.[1] Just now it was like the valley of Baca, that is, the Vale of Tears or Lamentation; but it has become a well—a fountain of universal joy.[2] When God brought David out of the horrible pit, out of the miry clay, and set his feet upon a rock, and established his goings, then He put a new song into his mouth, even praise unto our God. And what then? Did the blessed work stand alone? Nay, many saw, and feared, and trusted in the Lord.[3]

[1] Is., li. 3. [2] Ps. lxxxiv. 6. [3] Ps. xl. 1–3.

In what mournful contrast was David's experience in that saddest year of his life—the year of unconfessed guilt and a stupid conscience! He no more drew water with joy out of the wells of salvation.[1] Day and night God's hand was heavy upon him, and his moisture was turned into the drought of summer.[2] Rust gathered on his harp-strings, and the palace no more resounded with his morning and evening song.

And what was the result? It was then as now. The guilty Christian is the dumb Christian, and the dumb Christian is useless. Guilt paralyzed his tongue and sealed his lips. He could not teach transgressors the ways of God, and sinners were no more converted by his instrumentality.[3]

At length the voice of God broke the dismal silence. By His prophet and His providence,[4] He both rebuked and chastened him, until he came bending and weeping to the altar, and laid on it his broken spirit—that ever acceptable sacrifice, yea all sacrifices in

[1] Is., xii. 3. [2] Ps. xxxii. 4. [3] Ps. li. 13–15.
[4] 2 Sam., xii. 1–23. [5] Rev., iii. 19.

one.[1] In the Fifty-first Psalm you may read his confession, and in the Thirty-second the history of the whole matter—the guilty silence, the sore chastening, the ingenuous acknowledgment, the free pardon, and the overflowing thankfulness, confidence and joy. Nor does he fail to express his assurance that the usual result shall follow—that, because of his forgiveness and blessedness, so obtained, every one that is godly shall be encouraged to pray.

Ebenezer! Hitherto hath the Lord helped us.[2] Let gracious souls, who have fallen and been lifted up, who have sinned and found pardon, who have wrestled hard and overcome, be led to solemn and timely declarations of their Redeemer's grace. It is at once a debt of love and a deed of mercy.

> "Some forlorn and shipwrecked brother
> Seeing, shall take heart again."

Blessed Paul says he was before a blasphemer and a persecutor and injurious; but his Lord's grace was abundant; and it is a faithful

[1] Ps. li. 17. [2] 1 Sam., vii. 12.

saying, and worthy of all acceptation, that Christ Jesus came into the world to save sinners, of whom Paul felt himself to be chief. Howbeit, for this cause he obtained mercy, that in him first, Jesus Christ might show forth all long-suffering *for a pattern* to them which should hereafter believe on Him to everlasting life.[1]

This is one great end of a public profession of religion. We confess Christ that we may commend Him. The Church is a golden candlestick, which Christ has set on high to give light to a dark world.[2] When a new light is kindled, how shall it not covet to be set there too? Christ has commanded it, and can we refuse? He means it for beauty and for order; for our honor and defence; for a guide to the lost, an encouragement to the fearful, a testimony and rebuke to the carnal; for the comfort of the faithful; and for His own glory.

Yet let us not exalt our grateful telling above His gracious working. If the multitude had not seen what Jesus did, little would

[1] 1 Tim., i. 13–16. [2] Rev., i. 20.

they have minded what Bartimeus said. Their song began quicker and rose higher for his joyful key-note; still, it was of the miracle they sung. They waited only for proof that he actually saw, and when his rapturous outburst gave *that*, their hearts flowed over. And so our professions are nothing, except as true displays of Christ's work. Their virtue is in their verity—theii *transparency*, suffering the grace and power of God to shine through them. They bring glory to God as they are clear instances, and so proofs, of His Almighty, healing love.

How profoundly interesting and suggestive is this whole scene! Jesus has just wrought a work in which He has destroyed one of the works of the devil, redeemed a wretched man from his captivity and torment, and thereby brought glory to the Father; and now we behold Him serenely walking at the head of a vast multitude, who fill the air with acclamations at the gracious deed.

It is an epitome of His work on earth, and a foreshowing of His reward in heaven.

He came down from heaven, not to do His own will, but the will of Him that sent Him.[1] This was His meat,—that without which He could not live.[2] He sought not His own glory.[3] His Incarnation was for three great ends—the destruction of the devil and his works;[4] the salvation of the lost;[5] and the manifestation of the Father.[6] But the last was the great end, to which both of the others were subordinate. His whole life, His whole death breathed out this prayer, Father, glorify Thy name! He Himself announces this as the sum of all He had done on earth. It was on the night of His betrayal, but a few days after this triumphal march from Jericho, but a few hours before His death. Then the thirty-three years of His life on earth passed in solemn review before Him. They were indeed covered with obloquy and ignominy, but they presented nothing for regret. No repentance mingled with the contemplation, but rather, calm, deep, sublime satisfaction. Sur-

[1] John, vi. 38.
[2] John, iv. 34.
[3] John, viii. 50.
[4] Heb., ii. 14; 1 John, iii. 8
[5] Mat., xviii. 11.
[6] John, i. 18; xii. 27, 28.

rounded by chosen witnesses of His work and representatives of His Church, He lifted up His eyes to heaven, and exclaimed, I have glorified Thee on the earth, I have finished the work which Thou gavest Me to do.[1] It was for this He labored, for this He suffered; for this He saved, for this He destroyed. Zeal for His Father's glory absorbed Him,[2] consumed Him,[3] and yet sustained Him.[4] And it was only when this end was accomplished, as far as was possible in His estate of humiliation, that He thought of His own glory, and prayed to be restored to it—His essential, eternal, incommunicable glory, that which He veiled so deeply when He undertook His lowly errand. And *now*, O Father, He prays, glorify Thou Me with Thine own Self, with the glory which I had with Thee before the world was![5] O what a life was His! a whole consecration, all worship, all praise, one golden censer, full of divinest incense, ever burning and sending forth its fragrant clouds to heaven!

[1] John, xvii. 4. [2] John, iv. 34. [3] John, ii. 17.
[4] John, xii. 27, 28. [5] John, xvii. 5.

Finally, from this highway to Jerusalem and the hallelujahs of its festal multitudes, our thoughts are borne forward and upward.

> "There all the heavenly hosts are seen,
> In shining ranks they move!"

Bartimeus is there. Yea, every one of all that countless throng was once a poor Bartimeus, blind, wretched, ruined, the helpless captive of Satan, marred and accursed, until Jesus passed by to pity and to heal. And so each one is in turn the subject of the song and joy of all the rest.

The multitude is there. Now there is no chiding nor strife among them. They are without spot, or wrinkle or any such thing.[1] They "shine in the light of God," and have been made perfect in love.[2] They are all clothed in bright raiment of holiness and righteousness, and can look full upon the sunshine of the Throne. They wear crowns upon their heads,[3] and have harps and palms in their hands.[4] This is the sacramental host of God's

[1] Eph., v. 27.
[2] 1 John, iv. 18.
[3] 1 Pet., v. 4.
[4] Rev., vii. 9; xiv. 2.

elect, the general assembly and church of the first born.[1] An innumerable company of angels[2] is also with them, rejoicing in their joy, helping them to praise.

And Jesus is there. What would all this be without Him? Nay, without Him, none of this could be. The music would hush and the light go out. The crown would fall from the head, and the gold become dim.[3] Silence, coldness and death would cover the heavenly plains. But there He is, walking at the head of all the glorious company. He has loved them with an everlasting love,[4] and redeemed them at an infinite cost,[5] and now He sees of the travail of His soul and is satisfied.[6] It is finished! He presents them before His Father; "Behold I, and the children which God hath given Me!"[7]

"O long expected Day begin!"

---

1 Heb., xii. 23. 2 Heb., xii. 22.
3 Lam., iv. 1. 4 Jer., xxxi. 3.
5 1 Pet., i. 18, 19. 6 Isa., liii. 11.
7 Heb., ii. 13.

THE END.

SUNDAY SCHOOL BOOKS,

PUBLISHED BY SHELDON, BLAKEMAN & CO.

GLIMPSES OF JESUS; or, Christ Exalted in the Affections of his People. By the Rev. W. P. Balfern, of England. Large 18mo. 267 pages. Price, 60 cents.

This is an excellent book for young converts and inquiring minds.

THE ALMOST CHRISTIAN.

By Rev. Matthew Mead. With an Introduction by W. R. Williams, D. D. 18mo. Price, 45 cents.

"FATHER CLARK;" or, the Pioneer Preacher. By an Old Pioneer. 1 vol., 18mo. Gilt, muslin. Price, 60 cents.

"The adventures of John Clark, in early life, were more wonderful than fiction."—*Philadelphia Christian Observer.*

MEMOIR OF THE REV. THOMAS SPENCER. By Thomas Raffles, D.D., LL.D., his Successor in the Pastoral Office. With an Introduction and a Steel Portrait. 1 vol., 12mo. Cloth. Price, 50 cents.

THE SANCTUARY: Its Claims and Power. By W. W. Evarts, D. D. 1 vol., 18mo. Price, 50 cents.

THE LITTLE COMMODORE.

By May Rambler. With Eight Beautiful Illustrations. 300 pages. Large 18mo. Price, 75 cents.

www.ingramcontent.com/pod-product-compliance
Lightning Source LLC
LaVergne TN
LVHW010244110826
845151LV00004B/1385
9781425523398